# MAFIA HITS

# MAFIA HITS

## 100 MURDERS THAT CHANGED THE MOB

M. A. FRASCA

ARCTURUS

Dedicated to my dear mother and father,
Aunt Mary, Fazeena and Ed.

ARCTURUS

This edition published in 2016 by Arcturus Publishing Limited
26/27 Bickels Yard, 151–153 Bermondsey Street,
London SE1 3HA

ISBN: 978-1-78428-243-1
DA004799US

Printed in China

# CONTENTS

# CHAPTER 4

## CHAPTER 5
### THE SEVENTIES: TAKING CARE OF BUSINESS

## CHAPTER 6
### THE EIGHTIES: THE LAW FIGHTS BACK

# CHAPTER 7
## THE NINETIES TO TODAY: MODERN TIMES

# INTRODUCTION

*"You live by the gun and the knife and you die by the gun and the knife."* — Mob informant Joe Valachi to the McClellan Committee, 1963

The Mafia, or Cosa Nostra, first appeared in North America in the late 19th century, when gang members arriving from Italy, especially Sicily, settled in New York, Chicago and other urban centres, bringing their criminal ways with them. Loansharking, extortion, kidnapping, racketeering—they did it all and their reach was growing. It wasn't long before these gangs were clashing with each other and with existing Jewish and Irish mobs as the newcomers gained a firm foothold in the New World.

The 1920s brought Prohibition and an unexpected windfall for the mobs. There was money—lots of it—to be made from the illegal transportation and sale of liquor in the United States. America was dry and the mobs were eager to provide. Crime was bigger business than ever before and even the authorities were prepared to turn a blind eye in order to get their take. Criminals such as Jack "Legs" Diamond and Al Capone seemed to call the shots, but it was Lucky Luciano who became the pre-eminent mob boss and who created the Commission, the ruling body that to this day oversees all mob activity and disputes, thereby reducing in-fighting. It was also Luciano who divided the New York Mafia into five families and was shrewd enough to work with the Jewish and Irish mobs, making crime more efficient and truly organized.

It took a while for law enforcement officials to move effectively against the Mafia, some apparently not even realizing—or not admitting publicly—that the organization existed. It wasn't until 1957, when police broke in on a high-level mob meeting taking place in Apalachin, New York, that the existence of the Mafia was unquestionably verified, with further confirmation provided by mobster Joe Valachi in 1963.

Following the creation of the Racketeer Influenced and Corrupt Organizations (RICO) Act in 1970, strong initiatives have been put in place to curb the power of the Mafia. Despite this, it remains a powerful force today, controlling organized crime operations in New York, Chicago and Montreal in particular. But the success of the Mafia would not have been possible without the ruthless methods that the crime bosses employed. Albert "Mad Hatter" Anastasia, Benjamin "Bugsy" Siegel, "Big Paul" Castellano—the list of Mafia victims seems endless. *Mafia Hits* lists the most important executions—the rival bosses, the informers, the feuds, even some of the hit-men implicated in the assassination of President Kennedy. They're top of the lists of the "made men", the associates and freelancers who paid the ultimate price.

# 1

# THE NINETEENTH CENTURY: EARLY HOODS AND STREET BRAWLERS

**Mobs proliferated in the major cities of nineteenth-century America, but they generally acted independently and were constantly at war with each other. Organized crime was yet to come.**

Collusion between the gangs and political forces was marked, for politicians of all levels constantly used the brute force of the mobs in order to get ahead. The newspapers did the same thing, hiring gangs so they could muscle out the competition and expand their circulation.

Mobs such as the Five Points Gang and the Eastman Gang made life difficult for the average law-abiding citizen and honest cop alike. But there were other elements too. Black Hand extortion (used by Italian criminals preying exclusively on their fellow immigrants) was rife in cities, as was the more clannish Mafia itself.

Things were moving rapidly, however, as the century drew to a close. The old knuckle-busters were on their way out and mobsters such as Monk Eastman and "Kid Twist" Zwerbach were soon to take their final bows.

*The shooting of Chief of Police David Hennessey who had been investigating crimes connected with the Mafia in New Orleans, 15th of October 1890.*

# DAVID HENNESSY
## OCTOBER 16, 1890

## "MAFIA" BECOMES A HOUSEHOLD WORD

The murder of New Orleans Police Chief David Hennessy is considered to be one of the first recorded Mafia killings in America. Whether or not the Mafia was actually involved is unclear, but in the end it matters little—for it was the Italian population of the city that bore the brunt of Hennessy's death, on orders from the city's mayor, Joseph Shakspeare.

New Orleans during the late 1800s was a city of corruption and vice. Everyone was on the take, and that included officials. Even Shakspeare, who had been elected on an anti-corruption platform, was known to receive regular illicit payments from the gambling dens and brothels.

For years countless waves of immigrants had been pouring into the city, with Italians being currently bottom of the pecking order. Mixed in with these migrants were members of the Camorra and Mafia, who jostled for position in the city's underworld. Two rival families—the Provenzano and the Matranga—now vied for a piece of the criminal pie.

### ENTER CHIEF HENNESSY

Descriptions of Hennessy vary widely. He was either an honest cop trying to put a lid on the gang problem, or a crooked opportunist hoping to manipulate the underworld for his own purposes. Certainly Hennessy was no wallflower. Back in 1882 he had killed a rival officer in a shoot-out. The incident had cost him his job. Then, more recently as a crony of Mayor Shakspeare, he had not only found his badge reinstated, he had been appointed Chief of Police.

One of Hennessy's first tasks as chief of a force that was corrupt and riddled with political appointees was to lop off some of the dead wood. As a result, scores of lawmen lost their jobs. Next, he moved to crack down on the gambling dens and casinos—but only those not owned by members of Shakspeare's constituency. Evidently the clean-up went only so far.

Hennessy was also manoeuvring among the gangs. In an attempt to neutralize the more powerful of the two families—the Matranga—he had agreed to testify on behalf of the Provenzano if they promised to reveal all they knew about the Mafia.

### THE MURDER

Hennessy was never able to testify. On October 15, 1890, he was shot down on his way home. Lingering for about a day, he was able to provide only three words of information as to the identity of his killers: "Dagoes did it"—meaning the Italians.

But this was all Mayor Shakspeare needed to hear and he leapt at the chance to eliminate a painful thorn in his side. Immediately he ordered the police force to round up as many Italians as they could. Accounts differ as to how many were arrested in the witch-hunt, but figures range from 100 to 250—a number well beyond the "usual suspects". Only nine of these actually went to trial.

The trial was a fiasco from the start and both sides were accused of bribery and jury-tampering. In the end the judge had no alternative but to return an overall verdict of not guilty.

New Orleans was stunned. Agents of the mayor jumped on the soapbox and after a mass meeting the jail was stormed. When the smoke cleared, eleven prisoners were dead.

Yet even at the time opinion was divided as to who had actually killed Hennessy. Some dismissed Mafia involvement and believed the chief's death to be the work of either ex-lawmen or gamblers who had suffered as a result of Hennessy's clean-ups.

Nevertheless, anti-Italian sentiment lingered in New Orleans for years, with other ethnic Italians falling victim to the public mood. But the incident had further legacies too. The term "Mafia", once known only by a few, was now a household word. It's also said that because of the murders the American Mafia made it a hard and fast rule to never kill a cop. The price is just too high.

A group of men loitering in an alley known as 'Bandits' Roost', situated off Mulberry Street in New York City in 1888.

# MAX "KID TWIST" ZWERBACH
## MAY 14, 1908

### DEATH OF A LADIES' MAN

Born in Austria in 1882, Max Zwerbach was only two when the family emigrated to New York, hoping for a better life. Zwerbach's father had nurtured dreams of his two sons Maxwell and Daniel (later known as "Kid Twist" and "Kid Slyfox" respectively) joining him in the family tailoring business, an honest trade. Their nicknames give us a clue as to how little his dreams came true.

Max spent his youth in the slums of New York's Lower East Side. Living in poverty and amid crime, it's not surprising that he was soon getting into trouble. Petty offences such as bicycle theft and shoplifting escalated into more serious infractions and before long Max could be seen swaggering around town, the leader of his own fledgling gang.

A growing reputation for brutality and cunning brought Kid Twist to the attention of Monk Eastman of the ferocious Eastman Gang. As a strong-arm for the Eastmans, Kid Twist rose through the ranks, swiftly becoming one of Monk's second lieutenants alongside another hoodlum, Richie Fitzpatrick.

During this period the Eastmans tried to gain control of the Lower East Side, which meant bloody conflict with the Five Points Gang, headed by Paul Kelly (formerly Paolo Antonio Vaccarelli). But on February 3, 1904, Monk was arrested and

9

was soon on his way to Sing Sing prison. The Eastman Gang was left without a leader.

With Monk no longer around, Zwerbach and Fitzpatrick now went for each other's throats. And true to his name, Kid Twist managed to lure the gullible Fitzpatrick to a nearby bar to "discuss peace". Fitzpatrick didn't leave alive. Zwerbach was now head of the Eastman Gang.

### ENTER "LOUIE THE LUMP"

It was his amorous ways that would spell the end of Max "Kid Twist" Zwerbach. Despite being married, he had become entangled with Carroll Terry, a Canadian singer working in Coney Island's Imperial Music Hall.

Terry had once nurtured dreams of becoming an opera singer. But, alone in New York and with her funds depleted, she ended up living with Louis Pioggi, aka "Louie the Lump", a low-level thug in the Five Points Gang. At some time in 1908 Terry decided she'd had enough of the Lump and took up with Zwerbach.

But Pioggi was having none of it. On May 14, 1908, Kid Twist and his right-hand man, Vach Lewis (aka "Cyclone Louie", an ex-wrestler and sideshow strongman), set off for Coney Island to catch Terry's act. Running into Pioggi, Kid Twist and Cyclone started in on him, forcing him to jump from a second-storey window—only a two-storey fall, but still Pioggi's ankle was damaged. So was his pride.

After the show at around 8:30, Kid Twist, Cyclone Louie, Terry and her friend Mabel headed over to an Italian restaurant. Pioggi was waiting for them in the doorway. It took six shots to fell Cyclone Louie, ex-strongman that he was. Kid Twist received only one bullet, but this was a direct hit behind his right ear.

Terry survived to sing again, while Kid Twist dropped like a stone. He was only 24.

Legend has it that before the shooting Pioggi called Paul Kelly of the Five Points Gang, requesting permission to kill Kid Twist. Apparently a truck-load of Five Pointers showed up to assist Pioggi in the hit. Whether or not this was true, Max "Kid Twist" Zwerbach had been dealt with and was no longer a thorn in the Five Pointer's side. "Big" Jack Zelig took over the Eastmans after Kid Twist's demise and the gang was split into factions. By 1913 the Eastman Gang was gone.

# JOSEPH PETROSINO
## MARCH 12, 1909

### A TRUE CRIME FIGHTER

Joseph Petrosino was a legend of the NYPD. The co-chief, along with Antonio Vachris, of the force's Italian Squad, he had been promoted to the rank of detective sergeant by none other than future president Theodore Roosevelt. A celebrity in his lifetime, shortly after his death Petrosino was the subject of a feature film and serialized versions of his exploits appeared in the papers.

Petrosino was innovative in his methods. Making advances in police procedure, he used a network of informants to assist him and regularly went undercover to infiltrate the gangs. He is also credited with helping to initiate the NYPD's bomb and canine squads. More importantly, Petrosino was familiar with the plight of the average immigrant. He was one of them, he understood them. Petrosino knew only too well about the struggle against the Black Hand extortionists and the Mafia.

There are a lot of stories about Petrosino's exploits, some undoubtedly true. He backed down from nobody and once publicly thrashed the truly vicious Mafia assassin Ignazio "The Wolf" Lupo, humiliating him in full view of the street. After that, Lupo got in line behind the rest of the hoods who were queuing up to take a slice out of the detective.

In 1901, Don Vito Cascioferro arrived in the United States. A high-ranking and charismatic figure in the Sicilian Mafia, he was fleeing intensified scrutiny in Palermo. While in America the Don helped to fine-tune the American Mafia by improving its methods of extortion; his principle was never to extort too much money, as that way you could always come back for more. Cascioferro came to the attention of Petrosino after being implicated in the gruesome murder of counterfeiter Benedetto Madonia, who had been found stuffed in a barrel. The Don was released on bail, but Petrosino's dogged tenacity drove him back to Sicily.

It was the run-in with Cascioferro that sealed Petrosino's fate. In 1909, now a Lieutenant, Petrosino arrived in Sicily on a secret mission calculated to put a dent in the operations of the Mafia both in Sicily and the United States. The only problem was that the Mafia knew what Petrosino was up to and had been trailing him from the moment he set foot in Europe. Although he realized he was a doomed man, he continued with his mission anyway.

### THE GARIBALDI GARDEN

On the evening of March 12, 1909, Petrosino headed to the Garibaldi Garden in the Piazza Marina to talk to an informant. Perhaps surprisingly, he went to the meeting unarmed. Petrosino stood with his back to an iron gate so that no one could approach him from behind, but as he talked to the informant, two men ran out of the shadows and shot him four times in the head and shoulder. The lieutenant crumpled to the ground, dead.

Don Cascioferro was of course arrested for the murder, but to no one's surprise he wasn't held long and his later admission to the killing only enhanced his reputation. Petrosino received a state funeral in Italy and another, more impressive one when his body reached the United States. The day of the funeral was declared a holiday for New Yorkers, so that citizens could bid Joseph Petrosino farewell. More than 200,000 of them turned up. With the death of the Lieutenant, the fight against organized crime had lost one of its greatest heroes.

# "BIG" JACK ZELIG
## OCTOBER 5, 1912

### DEATH OF A GANGLEADER

"Big" Jack Zelig was gunned down by petty hood "Boston Red" Davidson on October 5, 1912 while riding the Second Avenue streetcar. At the time, Zelig was leader of the Eastman Gang after the assassination of "Kid Twist" Zwerbach and the incarceration of Abe Lewis that ended his brief leadership. Clearly, the Eastman Gang was having its troubles.

Zelig was a brawler and big in every sense of the word. Standing over 6 ft tall, he was one of the most feared men in New York City and more than handy in a knife-fight. Born Zelig Lefkowitz on May 13, 1882, his upbringing wasn't the usual one for a hood; his family was fairly comfortable and he had been given every opportunity in his early life. But Zelig gravitated to the gangs of the Lower East Side anyway and by the time he was twenty in 1908 he was running the Eastmans.

The Eastmans specialized in extortion, gambling and mayhem, and for a while things ran fairly smoothly under Zelig. In 1912, however, the old Eastman/Five Point rivalry resurfaced and the streets sizzled with gang wars. Zelig himself was a casualty, receiving a dangerous shot to the head. Such was his endurance, however, that he survived the wound and, once out of hospital, headed to Hot Springs, Arkansas for a little R & R.

The Eastmans also acted as thugs for Charles Becker, one of

the most corrupt cops on the force. One of Becker's numerous money-making schemes was to skim profits from illegal gambling joints. One casino owner, the hapless Herman "Beansy" Rosenthal, was foolish enough to complain about Becker's activities to both District Attorney Charles Whitman and to the papers. Becker's constant graft was keeping people like him down, he said. What was an honest crook to do?

Several days later, on October 12, 1912, Rosenthal was dead.

Suspicion immediately fell on Becker. He was accused of contracting Zelig, who had sent his right-hand men, "Lefty Louie" Rosenberg, "Whitey Lewis" Seidenschner, Harry "Gyp the Blood" Horowitz and Francesco "Dago Frank" Cirofici to take care of Beansy. Zelig himself was conveniently absent from the city when all this was going down, but when he got back he was called as a witness in the trial against Becker.

Becker, of course, had a lot to lose and it was no coincidence that Zelig never made it to the trial.

## THEY ALL FALL DOWN

Some mob historians believe it was all a frame-up. Becker, they hypothesize, was innocent and Zelig was actually planning to testify on the cop's behalf and not against him. We may never know. Contacted by phone on October 5, 1912, Zelig was called to a meeting on 14th Street. It was while he was on his way, riding the 5th Avenue streetcar, that Zelig was shot behind the ear and met his death.

When the dust settled the Eastman Gang was in ruins. Not only was Zelig dead, Lefty Louie, Whitey Lewis, Gyp the Blood and Dago Frank had all been executed. Even Becker went to the chair—the only officer in the history of the NYPD to do so.

# 2 PROHIBITION: RUM RUNNERS AND BEER BARONS

**It's been said that Prohibition did more for organized crime than any other single event, and though historians still debate this today, there's undoubtedly some truth to the statement. What is uncontested is that the Volstead Act that took effect in 1920, banning the manufacture and sale of alcohol, opened the door to increased profits for all the gangs and kept that door nicely wedged open for more than ten years.**

Smart mobsters—and even the not-so-smart ones—quickly realized the money-making potential that was now available to them and acted accordingly. These were formative years for the big names. Gangsters such as Lucky Luciano, Bugsy Siegel, Meyer Lansky, Dutch Schultz and Al Capone were on the rise, and things in the world of the criminal gangs would never be the same.

# JAMES "BIG JIM" COLOSIMO
## MAY 11, 1920

### DIAMOND JIM

Big Jim Colosimo loved the high life. Diamond stick pins, linen suits, expensive food and fine music—he wanted it all. His restaurant on Wabash Avenue regularly entertained the elite of Chicago, blue bloods and criminals alike. Colosimo's had a lavish six-course meal for those who could afford the $1.50 price tag and offered patrons a floor show that featured both ragtime and opera. It's no wonder they called him "Diamond Jim". But Big Jim just got too comfortable, and by 1920 he was obsolete.

Credited with organizing Chicago's underworld and with initiating what would become known as the infamous Chicago Outfit, Colosimo started his criminal career in Chicago's First Ward, picking pockets and committing petty crimes. Like so many of his contemporaries, he ultimately branched out into gambling, racketeering and vice. Marrying into the business, Colosimo wed bordello madam Victoria Moresco in 1902 and the two of them expanded the prostitution aspects of his criminal empire, ultimately owning over 200 brothels.

But all this wealth brought some unwanted attention and in 1909 Colosimo became the victim of a racket that he'd employed frequently himself—Black Hand extortion, where a threatening letter featuring a drawing of a black hand demands payment if the victim is to avoid consequences such as bodily harm, kidnapping or murder. He knew the game, he knew he'd have to keep on paying or he could expect more threats and escalated violence. To counter this he brought in a torpedo from New York, Johnny "The Fox" Torrio. Torrio, Victoria's nephew, would subsequently import an addition of his own into Colosimo's organization—a fledgling gangster who went by the name of Al Capone.

Torrio took care of Colosimo's extortion problem in a most effective and permanent manner. Remaining in Chicago, he became Colosimo's right-hand man, adding immeasurably to the efficiency of The Outfit.

With Torrio effectively running the organization, Colosimo had the opportunity to pursue other interests and started frequenting his restaurant more often. He also began to spend more time with his new wife. By 1920, Colosimo had divorced Victoria and married a young singer, Dale Winter, who performed as a lyric soprano in his restaurant.

### THE ROARING TWENTIES

Colosimo's folly occurred in 1920, when Prohibition took effect. Torrio recognized the windfall that the "Noble Experiment", as it was called, would offer The Outfit and urged Colosimo to take advantage of the criminal goldmine. But Big Jim wasn't interested. The operation was fine the way it was; why risk things by branching out into the unknown?

Clearly Colosimo was in the way of progress. On May 11, 1920, he arrived at his restaurant, ostensibly to deal with a shipment of whiskey. It was there, as he was waiting, that Colosimo was gunned down by an unknown assailant. Collapsing onto the tiled floor, he died in the lobby of his own establishment. Though no arrests were made for the killing, it's believed that the assassin was Frankie Yale, also over from New York and acting on orders from Johnny

Torrio. With Colosimo's death, Torrio assumed complete control of The Outfit.

Colosimo's funeral, just like his life, was a big deal—one of those extravagant gangster send-offs associated with the 1920s. The cortège filed through the streets of Chicago, taking Big Jim past his beloved restaurant one last time, while mourners and the curious crowded the street. Diamond Jim was finally laid to rest in a stately mausoleum in Oak Woods Cemetery—and once he was gone, the door to Prohibition was kicked wide open by The Chicago Outfit.

# EDWARD "MONK" EASTMAN
## DECEMBER 26, 1920

## THE EASTMAN GANG

He was the last of the old-time gangsters—a thug who did things with brass knuckles, a notched club and a knife. During his time he was one of the most notorious and powerful mobsters in New York. Yet when Edward "Monk" Eastman was buried in 1920, he went as a hero, with full military honours.

Monk was a brute and looked the part. Slovenly in appearance, he had thick, heavy features, cauliflower ears and stringy unkempt hair. His body bore the scars of the numerous knife fights and gun battles he'd been in. And to top all this, Monk wore a bowler hat several sizes too small.

Called "Monk" because of his ape-like appearance, Eastman was the leader of the gang that bore his name. Making their money from opium, illegal gambling and the usual mayhem, the Eastmans blustered around New York's Lower East Side, butting heads with the rival Five Points Gang headed by Paul Kelly. They also worked for the politicos at Tammany Hall, coercing voters and stuffing ballot boxes.

Monk had numerous run-ins with the law, but he could generally rely on the intercession of his Tammany friends to get him out of a jam. By 1903, however, things had really begun to heat up with the Five Pointers. Gun battles erupted on the streets, and several innocent bystanders were killed. The politicians at

Tammany Hall were starting to get flak about it and washed their hands of the gangs.

So in 1904, when Monk was arrested for attempted robbery, there was no reprieve and he was sentenced to ten years in Sing Sing. He actually served five, but when he came out in 1909 things had changed. He had become addicted to opium and his old gang was now split into factions, none of whom wanted to share with their old boss. There was just no room for Monk in the new power structure.

With no alternative, Monk returned to petty crime—but when in 1917 the United States entered the Great War, he enlisted. No doubt he found fighting in the trenches a breeze compared to some of the street battles he'd participated in back home. At any rate, Monk was in his element and tales of his heroism circulated among the troops.

### BACK ON THE STREET

At the end of the war Monk was hailed as a hero, and it was generally thought that he'd turned over a new leaf. But that was no dice—Monk was Monk. In the early morning of December 26, 1920, after enjoying a Christmas dinner at a gathering where the booze flowed freely, Monk got into an argument with one of his companions in crime—Jerry Bohan, a crooked Dry (Prohibition) Agent, likely over money. Following Bohan out onto the street, Monk called the agent a rat. Bohan retorted by filling Monk full of lead. That was it for Monk Eastman.

The men of Monk's former regiment had not forgotten all the gangster had done for them, however. Chipping in for his funeral, the GIs of O'Ryan's Roughnecks gave Monk a military send-off, complete with uniformed escort. It could be said that with the entombment of Monk, the Eastmans were finally well and truly buried.

# UMBERTO VALENTI
## AUGUST 11, 1922

### D'AQUILA'S TOP GUNMAN

As an enforcer for gangleader Salvatore D'Aquila, Umberto Valenti had quite a reputation. In his time, it was said that he was responsible for more deaths in New York than any other man. Though this may have been journalistic hype, Valenti was not a man to be taken lightly. When he went up against Joe "The Boss" Masseria, however, Valenti clearly found himself in a different league.

Not much is known about Valenti's early life, other than the fact that he was born in Sicily in 1891. By 1914 he was deeply involved in Salvatore D'Aquila's gang—an offshoot of the old Giuseppe Morello mob.

D'Aquila had once been a captain for Morello, but had since moved on. When Morello went to prison in 1910, control of his operation fell to underlings Nicolo, Vincent and Ciro Terranova and Joe Masseria, with the two mobs frequently at odds. Masseria in particular was a wily customer, but whatever his plans they had to be put on hold because in 1916, he too went to jail. It was during this period that Valenti forged his reputation.

The year of 1920 was a good one for organized crime. Not only was it the first year of Prohibition, it was also when Morello and Masseria were released from jail. Both men were anxious to pick up where they'd left off and reaffirm their power base.

D'Aquila now had his old rivals to deal with again and decided to take some strategic action. Unsure of Valenti's loyalties, D'Aquila ordered him to prove himself by assassinating Morello and Masseria, as well as other high-ranking capos in the old Morello gang.

Valenti's first hit went well enough. On May 7, 1922, he assassinated two Morello bosses on the same day—Vincent Terranova and Silva Tagliagamba. Both men were killed easily enough, but when Valenti went after Masseria things started to unravel.

### ATTEMPTS ON THE BOSS

The following day Valenti tried to take down Masseria in the middle of the street. A battle erupted, with bullets ricocheting everywhere, and though no actual gangsters were killed, unfortunately several innocent bystanders were.

On May 9, Valenti tried again. As Masseria left his home, two gunmen opened fire. Masseria dodged their first volleys, ducking and weaving like a boxer. The killers continued firing and managed to put a couple of bullets through his hat. Cutting their losses, the hit men fled the scene, driving their get-away car through a group of union workers and killing two of them. Masseria, though dazed, was still alive.

With two attempts on Masseria's life ending in failures, Valenti's stock was plummeting. His intended victim, though, was gaining quite a reputation.

On August 11 Masseria retaliated. Calling Valenti to a meeting on 12th Street, Masseria said he was willing to talk peace. When Valenti arrived, however, it was patently obvious that there was to be no peace-talk. Hat in hand, Valenti fled down the street but was gunned down as he jumped onto the running-board of a taxi. He died a short while later.

Now, here's an interesting side note—a teenage witness to the killing described how one gunman stood out from the rest, calmly firing his gun at Valenti as he sprinted down the road. The story goes that it was Salvatore Luciano who coolly pulled the trigger that day, putting an end to Valenti's life. Salvatore would later be better known as Lucky—Lucky Luciano.

# NATHAN "KID DROPPER" KAPLAN
## AUGUST 28, 1923

### THE DROPPER GETS DROPPED

In his early years, Nathan "Kid Dropper" Kaplan used to run a "drop con". A wallet of phony money would be planted on the sidewalk. Dropper would "find" the wallet then, supposedly unable to spare the time to locate the owner and claim the reward, would sell it off to some likely mark eager to collect the reward for himself. Of course there was no real owner and the sucker would be stuck with a wallet full of worthless bills.

It was a simple scam, strictly kid stuff, and by the 1920s, Kaplan had most assuredly graduated to bigger things. He was one of the many who cut their teeth in Paul Kelly's Five Points Gang, along with his buddy Johnny Spanish, who was reportedly the first to use an automobile in a hold-up. Though today Kaplan is credited with running his own gang by around 1910, newspapers of the time refer to him as belonging to Spanish's gang. Regardless, Kaplan and Spanish would soon become the worst of enemies, supposedly over the affections of a woman.

In 1911 both Kaplan and Spanish were sent to prison for seven years each. When Kaplan was released in 1918, the Five

Points Gang was history but by this time Kaplan really did have his own mob, "Kid Dropper's Rough Riders", and was anxious to stretch his muscles.

### LABOUR DISPUTES

The newest racket of the day involved the labour unions, and the mobs hired out as strong-arms for both the unions and the businesses. "Labour slugging"—protection from strike-breakers—was big bucks at the time and it wasn't only Kaplan who was involved in the racket, but also his old enemy Johnny Spanish and Jacob "Little Augie" Orgen. Once again violence erupted in the streets, with Kaplan and Spanish especially locking horns. In 1919 Kaplan finally managed to eliminate Spanish, while Orgen was sent to jail on a charge of robbery. For a while, Kid Dropper was the only game in town.

The party couldn't last forever, and by 1923 Little Augie was out of prison. His gang had not been idle while their boss was incarcerated and consequently the "Little Augies" had formed quite a power base. Kaplan would need to watch his step.

In early August of 1923, Kaplan was arrested on the charge of carrying a concealed weapon. On August 28, he appeared at the Essex Market Court for arraignment. Before noon that day Kaplan entered a taxi that had arrived to transfer him out. He was surrounded by a police escort, who were prepared for any trouble. They weren't prepared for little Louis Cohen though, as he walked up behind the car and reached up to the back window. Standing on tiptoe, the diminutive Cohen fired blindly into the cab, hitting Kaplan twice and killing him. Cohen was a low-level thug for the Augies and if he'd been promised any kind of protection for pulling the trigger on

Kaplan, he was to be tragically disappointed. He got a minimum of twenty years in Sing Sing—and now that Kid Dropper had been dropped, Little Augie Orgen controlled the labour rackets.

A crowd gathers around gangster Dean 'Dion' O'Banion's flower shop in Chicago, after he was shot seven times with a .45-caliber automatic pistol on the 10th of November, 1924.

# CHARLES DEAN O'BANION
## NOVEMBER 10, 1924

### CAGNEY'S "PUBLIC ENEMY"

Charles Dean O'Banion was something of an enigma. He had been a choirboy in his childhood and as an adult went to mass every Sunday, dropped money in the poor box, and worked in his flower shop.

But make no mistake, O'Banion was also an audacious and flagrant criminal. A major player in Chicago during the Roaring Twenties, he was both associate and adversary of Johnny Torrio and Al Capone. Between the three of them they owned Chicago, and the other mobs—the Genna brothers included—had to be content with what was left. O'Banion was big news in his day, and it was largely him (and his lieutenant, Hymie Weiss) whom James Cagney was imitating when he hitched back his shoulders and curled his lips into that predatory baby-faced sneer in *The Public Enemy*. Seeing that look, the audience knew that murder would follow.

O'Banion ran the North Side of Chicago, with the gang's headquarters in his flower shop. Called Schofield's, it was the place the gangsters went to when buying those large floral tributes for their fallen comrades. The shop was a front, of course, but O'Banion came to love pottering among the plants and pruning the leaves.

In 1920, with the dawn of Prohibition, it had been Torrio's idea to divide the city among the gangs. The division would allow everyone to get their fair share, while keeping a potential powder keg under control. After all, there was money to be made, but only if everyone played the game.

The plan worked well enough until about 1923, when the various mobsters began to chafe under the arrangement. As the year progressed the Gennas were making serious inroads into O'Banion's territory, while he, always happy in a heist, started hijacking whisky deliveries meant for the other mobs. Still trying to keep a lid on things, Torrio ceded O'Banion prime turf in the South Side, also throwing in a share in his nightclub, The Ship, to sweeten the deal.

But the capper came in 1924. Spending some time at The Ship, O'Banion learned that "Bloody" Angelo Genna had racked up a whopping gambling bill of over $30,000. Capone was inclined to let the matter drop, but not O'Banion. Supposedly, he got on the phone to Angelo and demanded payment of the debt within the week. It was an affront to the Genna boss, but it also made a handy excuse to force the issue. A vote was taken and the mobsters were unanimous—O'Banion would have to go.

It happened in the flower shop. O'Banion was there that day in the back room, preparing wreaths for recently deceased mob "fixer" Mike Merlo. The memorials were expensive and O'Banion had been asked to oversee them himself. He wasn't overly surprised then when the bell rang and three men, one of whom is believed to have been enforcer Frankie Yale, entered the shop. One of the men took O'Banion's hand in a fraternal grasp, then wouldn't let go. He was trapped, while the two other men drew their guns and shot him in the chest and throat. He died almost instantly.

With the murder of O'Banion, Chicago exploded in one of the bloodiest gang wars in mob history.

# SALVATORE "SAMOOTS" AMATUNA
## NOVEMBER 13, 1925

### THE AMBITIONS OF AMATUNA

Dean O'Banion was dead and gone—but that didn't mean the end of the North Siders, not by any stretch of the imagination. The North Side Gang, now under the leadership of Hymie Weiss, was about to take a very sharp knife and run it down the belly of Chicago. A wound like that would be pretty deadly; in fact it would mean the end of a lot of gangsters. Salvatore "Samoots" Amatuna would be one of them.

During the battle of Chicago, half of O'Banion's old enemies—the Terrible Gennas—had either been murdered, or had fled to New York. For a while—a very short while—leadership of the limping remnants of the Genna gang fell to Amatuna, a Sicilian-American gangster with aspirations to be head of the Unione Siciliana, a supposed cultural and beneficent group that had developed deep criminal connections.

Amatuna was a cut above the usual gangster, and definitely added a much-needed touch of class to the brutish Genna clan. For one thing, he understood the importance of good public opinion. After all, it didn't cost Amatuna much to buy his companions a suit when he was having one made up for himself, or to treat the street kids to a haircut when he visited the barber.

People tend to remember little touches like that. They take the sting away when it's time to draw a gun.

The Unione Siciliana was the linchpin in Amatuna's bid for power. Leadership of the Unione would give him control of more than the Genna gang. It would also give him clout with Al Capone and Jonny Torrio in the South Side, as well as the average (and beleaguered) Italian immigrant who had made his way to the city in hopes of a better life.

## BIG PLANS

So Amatuna—handsome and debonair—was about to make an alliance by marrying Rose Pecorara, the sister-in-law of past Unione president Mike Merlo. Though Merlo was dead by then, he had been one of the most honoured leaders of the Unione, a man both respected and beloved. Amatuna, who was by now the Unione president, had great plans—but they were never to be realized.

On November 10, 1925, Amatuna was getting his hair cut in a barber shop when two men burst in and shot the place up. Amatuna was hit and though he didn't die right away, it was only a matter of time. At the hospital, Rose by his side, Amatuna hoped to hold out long enough to wed his fiancé. But it was not to be. By the time the priest arrived, it was too late for marriage. Instead Amatuna received the last rites.

There is a picture of Salvatore Amatuna, one of the few known to exist, showing the man in the morgue, a mortician's number on his chest. Salvatore's eyes are open, and his lips are pursed. It's a picture of the man and of the quashed dreams of Salvatore "Samoots" Amatuna.

# HYMIE WEISS
## OCTOBER 11, 1926

### RETRIBUTION COMES

Henry Earl J. Wojciechowski, or Hymie Weiss as he was better known, is said to have been the only man that Al Capone ever feared. It was the 1920s and Chicago was rife with criminality derived from Prohibition. The city had been divided into sections, with Johnny Torrio and Al Capone running the South Side and the Genna brothers controlling Little Italy. Until recently, the North Side had been helmed by Dean O'Banion. But O'Banion was dead and Weiss, O'Banion's friend and lieutenant, was determined that someone was going to pay.

The North Siders were an extremely loyal bunch and Weiss in particular had a gallant side. The gang, for instance, shunned the prostitution rings that the other mobs found so lucrative. Weiss had a vile temper, though, one that could explode without warning. Because of the frequent debilitating migraines he experienced, it's now believed that he was suffering from cancer. Weiss's agony no doubt led to the wild outbursts that he was known for.

Perhaps aware that he was ill, Weiss may have decided he had nothing to lose in going after the South Siders and the Gennas. The mayhem started immediately and for several years Chicago bled.

## THE HEADLINES TOLD THE TALE

The crime reporters of the time had a field day. Headlines on mob warfare in 1925 alone included:

- January 24—Johnny Torrio, wounded by Weiss, heads to Italy, leaving the South Side gang to Capone.
- May 27—Angelo Genna is killed by North Siders Bugs Moran and Vincent Drucci.
- June 13—Mike Genna is shot down by police.
- July 8—Antonio Genna is murdered in the street.

As a result of all this, the surviving Gennas headed to New York, while the residue of their gang was taken over by Salvatore Amatuna then Joe Aiello, enemy of Capone. More telling, Capone increased his security. On August 10, 1926, Weiss and Drucci battled it out with Capone men at the Standard Oil Building, while September 20, 1926 brought another bold attack, this time at Capone's headquarters at the Hawthorne Inn.

Capone was now ready for a truce and had a delegate, Tony Lombardo, meet with Weiss and Bugs Moran. Capone himself did not attend the meeting, but participated over the phone.

At first the meeting seemed productive enough, with Capone offering Weiss territory in the South Side. But Weiss's demands were high; he expected nothing less than two of the murderers of Dean O'Banion—Albert Anselmi and John Scalise. So far, Anselmi and Scalise had done nothing that could be construed as being disloyal to Capone, so his reply to Weiss on that matter was brief and to the point—he wouldn't do that to a dog. With that, the conference was at an end.

Deciding that it was now time, Capone ordered Weiss's assassination. The hit was meticulously planned. Capone's men rented the building next to the North Side hangout—Schofield's Flower Shop—in preparation. This was the very place where O'Banion had met his demise. Other locations were rented across the street from the shop, giving the gunmen optimum vantage points. On October 11, 1926, when Weiss arrived at Schofield's, along with North Side ally Patrick Murray and several others, the gunmen opened fire. Murray was killed instantly and Weiss, hit several times, collapsed. He died on his way to the hospital.

Weiss was buried not far from his pal Dean O'Banion, and with his death the North Siders were inherited by Drucci and Moran. But it wasn't over—not by a long shot—and the battle for Chicago continued.

# JACOB "LITTLE AUGIE" ORGEN
## OCTOBER 16, 1927

### THE LITTLE AUGIES

Jacob "Little Augie" Orgen and his gang were labour sluggers—hoods hired out as muscle both to the unions and to the corporations during labour disputes. Pictures of Orgen show him with a prominent scar on his left cheek, just below the eye. The mark looks like one of those duelling scars that military officers from a previous generation used to sport. The difference was that Orgen had been awarded his wound in a street fight.

The Little Augie Gang shared the labour rackets in New York with Johnny Spanish and, of course, Nathan "Kid Twist" Kaplan. Kaplan eliminated Spanish in 1919, the same year that Orgen went to prison, and Orgen in his turn dealt with Kaplan in 1923, subsequently assuming control of New York's union rackets.

### MURDER INC.

The Little Augies contained a number of up-and-comers in the underworld, including such criminal luminaries as Louis "Lepke" Buchalter, Jacob "Gurrah" Shapiro and Jack "Legs" Diamond. Diamond was to become quite a celebrity in the 1920s, but Buchalter and Shapiro would prove more formidable. Buchalter, a shrewd tactician, would later expand his resumé when he assumed leadership of the National Crime Syndicate's murder wing—Murder Incorporated.

By the mid 1920s, however, the labour rackets were beginning to change. Orgen had his hand in other things of course, bootlegging included, but found that membership in the unions had begun to drop. What's more, the fear of Bolshevism was leading to increased scrutiny of all labour movements. This extra attention was beginning to shine a spotlight on the gangs, and that was something no one wanted.

Arnold "The Brain" Rothstein—mob ruler, gambler and brilliant strategist—urged the Orgen gang to use a tactic of infiltration instead. Working inside the unions, he advised, would allow for more subtle control of labour, give Orgen access to union coffers and still allow for a hefty pay-off from the corporations. The gambit would also have greater benefits in the long run than simple labour-bashing, which could only ever be effective for a while.

The plan appealed to Buchalter and Shapiro, both protégés of Rothstein, but Orgen liked to do things the old-fashioned way by knocking heads together. Clearly the gang could have no future with Orgen in charge and in any case, the wily Buchalter had plans of his own.

On October 16, 1927, Orgen was walking down Norfolk Street, accompanied by Jack Diamond as bodyguard. As the two neared Delancey a car pulled up beside them, a window opened, and Buchwalter and Shapiro filled Orgen with lead. Diamond was also hit but managed to survive, fuelling his later reputation as the man who could not be killed.

Buchwalter and Shapiro now had control of Orgen's operations. Many years later, however, Buchwalter's own number would come up when he went to the electric chair in 1944.

# FRANCESCO IOELE (FRANKIE YALE)
## JULY 1, 1928

## CAPONE'S FIRST BOSS

He's the guy who gave Al Capone his first job—Francesco Ioele, better known as Frankie Yale. Though based in New York, Frankie also did favours for Capone and Johnny Torrio in Chicago; it was Yale who bumped off both Big Jim Colosimo and Dean O'Banion for his Chicago pals. But in 1928, when Yale crossed Capone, he found he'd made a grave error.

Yale was a crime boss and enforcer and like so many other mob figures, though he could be generous, he was an extremely violent man. He once brutally beat his own brother and is considered responsible for the decapitation of crime boss Ernesto Melchiorre. Of course by the 1920s Yale had expanded his operations into labour racketeering, extortion and bootlegging. He even marketed a "Frankie Yale" brand of foul-smelling cigars that he forced shopkeepers to sell.

The friction between Capone and Yale started around 1925. In that year Capone successfully backed Tony Lombardo for the leadership position of the Unione Siciliana. Lombardo instituted some reforms within the Unione which probably cost Yale some graft. In retaliation, Yale put his backing behind Joe Aiello, a rival of Capone.

By 1927 the situation had deteriorated to such an extent that Yale felt it was time to teach Capone a lesson. Yale used to act as a rumrunner, bringing shipments of booze from Canada into the United States. The liquor would then be sent off to supply some of the other gangs, Capone's included, with hooch they could sell to the speakeasies in their territories. In the spring of '27, however, some of the shipments meant for Capone began to vanish.

Capone smelled a rat. Sending in James D'Amato to infiltrate the gang and investigate the missing shipments confirmed Capone's suspicions—Yale himself was responsible for the hijackings. To make matters worse, once Yale discovered D'Amato's treachery, he had him killed.

There was nothing now that could save Yale. On July 1, 1928, while sitting in his bar, he received a mysterious call requesting that he return home immediately. The caller must have been persuasive, because Yale leapt up and jumped into his car. As he sped along New Utrecht Street, a car containing four men pulled up alongside him. The occupants, rolling down their windows, opened fire on Yale. Flooring the accelerator and careening down 44th Street, Yale lost control of his car and smashed into the front of a house. With his body spilling out onto the street amid the broken glass and twisted steel, Frankie Yale was dead.

### TOMMY GUNS

The Thompson submachine gun that was used to dispatch Yale was later found in an abandoned car. The killing marked the first time that a submachine gun had been employed in a New York gangland war, though it was already gaining popularity in Chicago, where it was referred to as a "Chicago Typewriter".

The use of a tommy gun in Yale's death was deliberate on Capone's part and was intended to send a message to the New York underworld. When the gun was found, there would be mistaking where the hit on Frankie Yale actually came from—it was Chicago style.

# ARNOLD "THE BRAIN" ROTHSTEIN
## NOVEMBER 6, 1928

### THE FIXER

Arnold Rothstein was known as "The Fixer", as well as "The Brain". It was he who had first realized the potential that Prohibition offered the underworld, passing that notion on to Johnny Torrio, in particular. It was Rothstein too who first understood that crime would be most effective if run along the lines of a corporation—in the end it's always better to get things done through bribery than through violence.

Rothstein was a gambler and he'd made his first million through betting, casinos and loansharking. He wasn't above stacking the deck, though, and if a bet wasn't a sure thing, then he'd make it that way. To that end, Arnold had been known to tamper with horse races and had also been accused of fixing the World Series, a revelation that shocked the nation back in 1919.

Rothstein's father had been a respectable businessman and philanthropist. As a result, his son was educated and well-read. He had connections that ran deep in business and political arenas and he "owned" more than a few politicians—it was how he got things done. Known as a fixer, he would arbitrate rivalries between the mobsters, and had soon expanded his operations to include speakeasies, labour infiltration, bootlegging and then narcotics. His

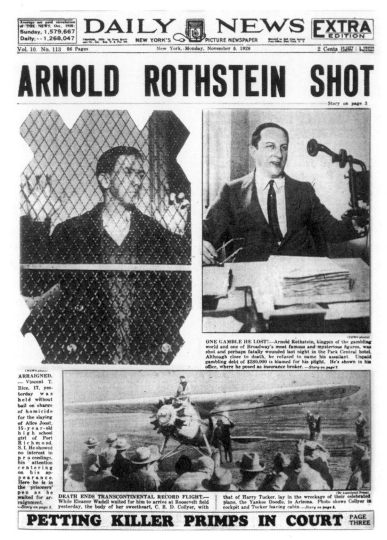

Daily News *front page, 5th of November, 1928, reporting the fatal shooting of Arnold Rothstein at the Park Central Hotel, Manhattan.*

organization included criminal heavy-hitter Lucky Luciano and he mentored Meyer Lansky, both of whom owed much of their take on organized crime to Rothstein's progressive ideas, rather than to the primitive blood-and-guts methods of the earlier crime lords. But it was gambling that Rothstein loved best and he would put money down on anything from the ponies to political elections.

## A BAD BET

It was fitting, then, that gambling would cost Rothstein his life. In late October of 1928 he had participated in a marathon poker game, lasting several days. But as the game progressed, something seemed slightly wrong; Rothstein, playing at first with his usual luck, had hit a dry spell and just couldn't get back on track. His fortunes had lately taken a setback, and he had lost a considerable amount of cash on a bad racetrack bet while his narcotics operation had been bleeding money. During this game, the bad luck continued and Rothstein had raked up quite a debt—over $350,000, in fact. When the game ended, Rothstein refused to pay, claiming the game had been fixed.

On November 5, 1928, Rothstein was called to a meeting at the Park Central Hotel. Shortly afterwards he staggered from the room with a bullet wound to his abdomen. He lingered for a day, but avoided naming his killer. A fellow gambler, George McManus, was tried for the murder, supposedly committed because of Rothstein's refusal to pay off his debt. He was later acquitted.

It has been suggested that Rothstein's killer could have been Dutch Schultz, Meyer Lansky or Lucky Luciano, each of whom stood to gain by his downfall. The theory has some weight. After all, how could McManus hope to collect a debt from a dead man?

# ST. VALENTINE'S DAY MASSACRE
## FEBRUARY 14, 1929

### THE BIGGEST HIT OF 'EM ALL

It is a snowy morning, February 14, 1929. Seven men—most of them members of George "Bugs" Moran's North Side Gang—gather inside a garage in Chicago's Lincoln Park area, apparently awaiting the arrival of a truck of bootleg whisky. The location is a known hangout for the gang.

At approximately 10:30 a.m. a squad car pulls up in front of the garage. Two men wearing police uniforms and carrying guns step out. They enter the garage and demand Moran's men drop their weapons and face the wall—this is a raid. The "policemen" then open a back door and let in more men, these ones dressed in suits, ties and hats and also carrying weapons.

Shortly after that the armed group opens fire on Moran's gang. Both machine guns and rifles are used in the bloody attack, and over 70 rounds of ammunition are sprayed into Moran's men and into the back wall.

The job done, some of the killers exit through the rear door of the garage. But the rest—the two "policemen" and two of the "civilians"—leave through the front entrance. The civilians are being forced out at gunpoint, their hands raised as if under arrest. To any onlookers it appears that the police have matters well in hand.

Alarmed by the commotion, Jeanette Landesman, ironing clothes in a nearby boarding house, sends over a lodger to investigate. The lodger returns a short while later, ashen-faced, and tells Jeanette to call the police—something terrible has happened.

When the real police arrive, they find a gruesome site. The St. Valentine's Day Massacre, as it is later dubbed, is the bloodiest hit in Chicago mob history, and unquestionably the most infamous gang assassination of all time.

Six of the victims die outright, but one—Frank Gusenberg—is miraculously still alive and trying to drag himself to the door. When asked by police who did it, Gusenberg refuses to talk. He dies three hours later.

There are no survivors and no one is brought to trial, but the chain of events seems clear. This hit is just the latest in the long line of skirmishes that Bugs Moran's North Side Gang and Al Capone's South Side Gang have been engaged in for years. The costs have been high on both sides. On that morning in February, Capone makes a bid for supremacy with an attack on Moran. The only problem is that Moran isn't there.

The investigation seems to drag on for years, with the police pursuing several leads, but strangely never following through. It is not until 1934 that a low-level hood—Byron Bolton—is able to fill in the details of what really happened on that St. Valentine's Day.

According to Bolton, in October or November of 1928 Capone and some of his men sat down at a Wisconsin resort and planned the hit, intending to kill Moran and several of his gang. The strategy was for Bolton to keep a look-out near the garage and alert the hit team, waiting at the Circus Café, the moment that Moran appeared. That morning, when a group of Moran's men arrived at the garage, Bolton mistook one of them for Moran. The target apparently spotted, Bolton gave the signal and the cars began to arrive.

## IT JUST WASN'T HIS TIME

But Moran was late in reaching the garage, and when he pulled up and saw a police car there he ducked into a coffee shop instead. Bumping into another of his men along the way, he told him to avoid the garage as it was being raided.

This mistake didn't really matter, though—the hit did the trick and Moran's operations were dealt a deadly blow. But it also brought a lot of unwanted attention to Capone, even though he was in Florida at the time and had an alibi. In 1930 Capone became Public Enemy Number One, and by the end of 1933 he was in jail serving an eleven-year stretch.

Dying in his bed in 1947, Capone had never again been able to regain the power he wielded during his Chicago heydays. And the famous Massacre wall, the one that the victims were facing when they were shot? It's now part of the Mob Museum in Las Vegas, minus a few souvenir bricks—gruesome mementoes.

# JOHN SCALISE AND ALBERT ANSELMI
## MAY 7, 1929

### THE MURDER TWINS

John Scalise and Albert Anselmi seemed to be joined at the hip. Though Anselmi was Scalise's senior by around seventeen years, the two Sicilians were inseparable, with Scalise being the dominant one of the pair.

Scalise arrived in Chicago in the early 1920s, while Anselmi came some time in 1924. Anselmi spoke no English and Scalise's knowledge of the language was limited, but that didn't matter; command of the language was not really required for the jobs the two were contracted to perform. Almost immediately, both men, though separately, attached themselves to the Genna Gang in Chicago. It was while working for the Gennas that the men formed their life-long friendship. From there they gravitated to Capone and the South Side Gang.

Once with Capone the pair honed their craft and were responsible (along with Frankie Yale) for the death of North Side crime boss Dean O'Banion. In fact it was the lives of Scalise and Anselmi that North Sider Hymie Weiss demanded in reparation for O'Banion's murder. Capone said no dice.

Throughout 1925 the battle between the South Siders and

the North Siders raged in the city of Chicago. In June of that year, Scalise and Anselmi, along with Mike Genna, waylaid and attacked North Siders Vincent Drucci and Bugs Moran. After a long battle and pursuit by the police, Genna was killed while several officers were also gunned down. The Murder Twins—as they came to be known—were taken into custody.

Over the next few years the pair went to trial twice for the murder of the officers. The original ruling sent them to jail for fourteen years, but they must have had a good lawyer and no doubt some political pull through Capone, because their case was retried and they were acquitted. To Scalise and Anselmi it must have seemed that they could get away with anything, including murder. Scalise even rose to the position of vice president of the Unione Siciliana under the presidency of Joseph "Hop Toad" Giunta.

### A PARTY TO DIE FOR

What happened next remains the subject of some controversy. Supposedly, while Scalise, Anselmi and Giunta were attending a gathering, a violent argument broke out and all three men were murdered. The party may or may not have been a ruse to lure them to their deaths.

But a more sensational version of the story has now become a part of the Capone legend, undoubtedly growing with each retelling. In this account, Capone bodyguard Frankie Rio happened upon the startling revelation that Scalise and Anselmi had planned on betraying and murdering Capone.

Turning the table on the pair, Capone threw an elaborate party in which Giunta was also in attendance. Apparently after an extravagant meal had been enjoyed, and speeches had been endured, Capone pulled out a baseball bat and proceeded to beat the trio mercilessly. That done, several underlings then drew their guns and finished the job.

Whatever the case, Scalise and Anselmi were dead and their remains were shipped back to Sicily for burial. The Twins had died together and now they were going home together.

# 3 THE DIRTY THIRTIES: CRIME GETS ORGANIZED

**The Dirty Thirties represented a high-water mark for the mobs. It was during this period that Charlie "Lucky" Luciano brought some order to underworld proceedings with the creation of the Commission (for the five New York Mafia families) and the Syndicate (for organized crime throughout the country, including the Mafia). In theory, all gang criminal activity was now to be overseen by these two groups. In other words, crime was organized.**

The 1930s also saw the creation of Murder Incorporated, run by Louis "Lepke" Buchalter, his buddy Jacob "Gurrah" Shapiro, and Albert "The Lord High Executioner" Anastasia. To keep things tidy, the murder group was to oversee a large number of the killings contracted by the Commission and the Syndicate. It's estimated that Murder Inc. was responsible for the death of approximately 1,000 people.

# ALFRED "JAKE" LINGLE
## JUNE 9, 1930

### FREEDOM OF THE PRESS

The last day in the life of Alfred Lingle reads like something straight out of a Hollywood movie. On July 9, 1930, he left the Sherman House Hotel and headed to catch the 1:30 p.m. train from Illinois Central Station to the Washington Park racetrack. Meeting a police friend along the way, Lingle told him that he felt he was being tailed. Despite this, he carried on to the Randolph Street Tunnel, a subway that leads to the train terminal. It was packed at that time of day. Lingle stopped to buy a racing form, while a priest mingled with the crowd. Unfolding the paper, Lingle looked up as two men in a car waved to him, calling out "Play Hy Schneider in the 4th." Two other men, one dark and one fair-haired, fell in step beside him.

As Lingle made his way through the tunnel, a cigar clamped in his mouth, the fair-haired man lifted a .38 and shot him in the back of the head. Pandemonium ensued. The killer bolted, discarding some grey gloves he'd been wearing. One witness started in pursuit of the blond gunman, but the "priest" who had been lounging in the station blocked his path.

The killer, unable to navigate his way through the crowd, was forced to double back past Lingle's body, the cigar still clamped in the lifeless mouth. Then, jumping over a guard-rail, he disappeared into the bushes.

This was quite an operation, one that reeks of a mob set-up, with at least five hit-men involved—a number that includes the strategically placed "priest" and the two men in the car who fingered Lingle to the killer. The murder was professionally planned and professionally carried out, and when it hit the papers, all hell broke loose.

## THE TRUTH WILL OUT

So, who was Alfred "Jake" Lingle? As far as the average citizen of Chicago was concerned, Lingle was simply a "legman" for the *Chicago Tribune*. Not actual reporters, legmen sniffed out hot crime stories, then phoned them in to the paper where a journalist could write them up.

Immediately after his murder, however, Lingle became something more than a legman. In death, he was transformed into a martyr, a symbol of the crusading newspaperman who had uncovered a story so sizzling that the mob—probably Capone—had to take him out. The papers even offered a $55,000 reward for Lingle's killers. A little while later, once things had cooled down a bit and some real journalists had done some digging, another side of Alfred Lingle began to emerge—one that was very different from a brave contributor to the press.

Though Lingle only made $65 a week, he had several huge bank accounts and expensive homes, along with taking luxury vacations in Cuba with his wife and children. He was known to make very large bets on the horses and eat at high-class restaurants and, most damning of all, he boasted one of those diamond-encrusted belt buckles that Al Capone liked to give his buddies. In fact, he was wearing it when he died.

Pennies began to drop everywhere—in fact there was a deluge of pennies. Lingle was not the upstanding, hard-hitting, crusading newspaperman that everyone thought he was. Lingle was a louse, a mob go-between who was playing several games at once. Tight friends with Police Commissioner William F. Russell, Lingle would give the mobs the heads-up whenever a raid was planned, or even get Russell to call off busts when it was advantageous; he would extort money from the gangs, threatening busts on speakeasies and clubs if he wasn't given a share of the profits; he would sell promotions to ambitious young police officers; and he was rumoured to own a piece of every barrel of liquor sold in Chicago. All of these schemes provided Lingle with a very healthy pay-off. It looks like he really earned that belt buckle from Capone.

So really, it could have been anyone who murdered Lingle— or at least anyone who could pull off a very professional job. After all the suspects were sifted through, police—and undoubtedly Capone as well—came to the conclusion that the mastermind behind Lingle's murder was undoubtedly ex-Capone man turned North Sider Jack Zuta. The reason probably had to do with the price Lingle was extorting for the reopening of a North Side property, the Sheridan Wave Club—but by the time the bulk of this had been revealed, the press had lionized him as one of their own going down in a blaze of glory and Lingle had received a funeral worthy of a war hero.

# JACK ZUTA
## AUGUST 1, 1930

### DANCE HALL DROP

As Jack Zuta sat in the Chicago Police Department, he must have been wishing that he could turn back time. Some days earlier, he had authorized the murder of Alfred "Jake" Lingle, a definite irritant in his side. Now the double-dealing Lingle was dead, but for some reason the press and public had decided to make a hero of him and the whole situation was getting way out of hand. What the heck was all the fuss about, Zuta must have wondered—Lingle was just a $65 a week legman as far as the public was concerned. To those in the know, of course, Lingle was an extortionist and a rat.

But Lingle had also been in pretty thick with the all-powerful Capone, and now here was Zuta stuck in the middle of Capone territory, enduring a police grilling. What's more, he had no safe way of making it back to his home turf.

Zuta—mob accountant and greaser that he was—always had his own interests at heart, so he begged for a ride back to the North Side from one of the cops who had picked him up in the first place—Lieutenant George Barker. Barker agreed, after a certain amount of wheedling on Zuta's part, and Zuta and three pals who had been picked up with him got into the lieutenant's car, Zuta cowering in the back seat.

Once they were in the car, though, the race was on. As Barker drove, another automobile pulled up beside him and one of the occupants—in true 1930s gangster style—jumped out onto the running board and started blasting away. Bullets hailed through the car windows, and Barker was forced to stop in order to return fire. It was a shoot-out in the street, and several innocent bystanders were wounded or killed. When at last it was all over, the attackers careened off, smoke spewing from an engine that had been specially modified to provide camouflage. Zuta, who had been slightly wounded, hobbled off briskly, losing himself in the crowd. But there was no doubt that Capone was royally upset.

Immediately Zuta made himself scarce and headed for a spa in Wisconsin. Here was a chance for him to relax, at least for a while. He could enjoy the scenery, listen to the music at the local dance palace, and watch the dancers cut a rug, all without the fear of Capone's goons showing up. Or so he thought.

### "GOOD FOR YOU, BAD FOR ME"

This blissful period of peace was excruciatingly short-lived, however. At the beginning of August, a witness at the local drugstore later testified that she heard Zuta using the store phone, and demanding that someone had better get up there damn quick to get him out of there—pronto! Later that very night, after the desperate call from the drugstore, Zuta put in an appearance at the local dance hall. Enjoying a drink of ginger beer and sitting next to the self-playing piano, Zuta began listening to music. Just as he dropped a coin into the machine and began to enjoy that jazzy number "Good For You, Bad For Me", the door to the dance palace burst open.

Later, such names as Dean Stanton and Tony Accardo—Capone men both—would be bandied about in connection with the incident. But that night most of the people in the establishment didn't know who the men were. All they saw were the guns—a machine gun, a rifle, and a number of pistols. No doubt they also watched as Jack Zuta was shot in the mouth, stood up and tried to run, then was pelleted with more gun blasts and collapsed dead on the floor.

Just as there was fall-out after the murder of Jake Lingle, so there was fall-out after the death of Jack Zuta. Zuta had kept meticulous records of all his mob transactions—everything from notes about bribes to civic officials to compromising photos of millionaires and politicians. The city, in fact, was aghast at the corruption that was uncovered when Zuta died.

But Al Capone? He got what he was after, and he wasn't going to let anyone forget it. In fact, one time, when he heard a bounty had been placed on his head Capone quipped, "Nobody's gonna Zuta me."

# GIUSEPPE MORELLO
## AUGUST 15, 1930

### "THE OLD FOX"

Giuseppe Morello, or "The Old Fox" as he was known, was an early mafioso operating in New York. Heading a gang originally referred to as the 107th Street Mob, he was one of the most powerful crime bosses of his day—the legendary *capo di tutti capi*, "Boss of all Bosses", in fact.

Morello had entered the Mafia while still in Sicily. Upon arriving in the United States, and eventually settling in New York, he brought the family business with him. Morello's gang liked to use the old Black Hand extortion racket—threatening violence on fellow Italians until a pay-off was made. But Morello also had a hand in smuggling and counterfeiting. He was arrested in 1900 for passing phony five-dollar bills which at the time were described as roughly executed and of poor quality. He later improved his counterfeiting process, however, and was able to pass near-perfect replicas. Morello would launder these phony bills through his restaurants, saloons and other establishments—one of the first crime bosses to launder money in this way.

Morello and his lieutenant, the deeply sinister Ignazio Lupo "The Wolf", were extremely dangerous individuals and were responsible for countless murders. Their specialty was the "barrel murder", so called because the victims would be stuffed into a barrel after death. None other than Joseph Petrosino had a run-in with the gang in 1903 while investigating the barrel murder of Benedetto Madonia.

In 1909 Morello and Lupo were sent to prison. Morello's original sentence was twenty-five years, but he only served about ten. Still it was a long stretch, and while in prison, of course, Morello had no way of exercising control of his gang.

### PICKING OFF THE TERRANOVAS

During his incarceration, the Morello mob, now overseen by Morello's half-brothers, the Terranovas, began to lose territory to rival gangs. In 1916 Nicolo Terranova was gunned down and when Morello was released from prison in 1920 he found himself also a marked man. Salvatore D'Aquila, at one time a subordinate Morello, currently owned much of the rackets in New York City. Now with his old boss released, he found that he was reluctant to relinquish the power that he had connived so long to amass.

D'Aquila ordered his gunman Umberto Valenti to eliminate Morello and his associates, including rising boss Joe Masseria. Valenti was only partially successful but was able to eliminate another of Morello's half-brothers, Vincent Terranova, and a few intermediate hoods before he himself was killed by Masseria.

Masseria now assumed control of the Morello gang, with Morello taking a subordinate position to his former underling. Now over sixty-three years old, Morello was a wily strategist, one who had seen his fair share of gang struggles, and his opinions were greatly respected. He assisted Masseria as he moved to consolidate his powerbase and to eliminate rivals, including Salvatore Maranzano of the Castellammarese, a faction that was backed by the Sicilian Mafia.

On August 15, 1930, Morello was killed as he worked in his East Harlem office. He was one of the first victims of what was to become the infamous and bloody Castellammarese War, a conflict which directly ushered in a new era of organized crime and the creation of the Commission (a ruling body for the Italian Mafia) and the National Crime Syndicate (the ruling body for all mobs).

# JOE AIELLO
## OCTOBER 23, 1930

### FIFTY-NINE BULLETS

Fifty-nine—that's the number of bullets they plugged into Joe Aiello in 1930. That definitely seems like overkill, but Aiello brought it all on himself. He just seemed to have a one-track mind and no matter what anyone else was talking about at the time, he would inevitably steer the conversation back to his pet subject—whacking Al Capone.

It's not as if Aiello didn't have enough to do without starting trouble with Capone. By 1925 he controlled the remnants of the Genna brothers' old gang, which brought in lots of dollars from the home-made stills of Chicago's Little Sicily; and in 1929 he finally realized his dream of becoming president of the Unione Siciliana. And that is the crux of the matter. Apparently Capone had backed Aiello's ex-friend Tony Lombardo in the bid for presidency of the Unione. After that move, Aiello seemed compelled to start yet another war in Chicago.

Aiello had comparatively little trouble when it came to taking out Lombardo. Capone, though, was a different matter. Here's a run-down of just a few of his attempts:

Early 1927: Aiello pays the chef at one of Capone's favourite eateries to put prussic acid into the big guy's soup. The chef tips off Capone, and the whole Borgia-like escapade falls apart.

Later in 1927: an Aiello machine-gun nest is discovered

*Mika Bizarro, Joe Aiello, Joe Bubine, Nick Manzello and Joe Russio, standing in front of a wall in a jail, Chicago, Illinois, 1927.*

directly across the street from Capone's favourite cigar store.

May 25 to September 24, 1927: a total of eight Aiello men or hirelings are butchered in the war. In desperation Aiello offers $50,000 for the head of Capone, but all that does is pile up more bodies on his own side.

April 1929: Aiello tries to use Capone gunmen Albert Anselmi and John Scalise to kill their boss. Capone's spies reveal the plot and the Murder Twins are killed instead.

### PROPAGANDA TACTIC

In 1927, when Capone found out that Aiello was being held at the South Clark Street police station on a weapons charge, he made a grand show of power, intended to put Aiello in his place; he sent down a goon platoon of twenty-five strong to make its presence felt at the courthouse and generally spread intimidation around in a broken-nosed kind of way. The press had a field day in expectation of a bloody shootout. Flashing their guns around, a couple of the gangsters were disarmed by the police, then hustled into the courthouse where they proceeded to put the fear of Al into Aiello.

The whole thing was getting very bloody—and costly. Just how many more men could Aiello afford to lose?

Finally, on October 23, 1930, Aiello decided to skip town for a little while, and was holed up in the house of the astonishingly named Pasquale "Patsy Presto" Prestogiacomo when the boom was finally lowered. With his bags packed, and supposedly on his way to Mexico City, Aiello was shot as he headed for a waiting cab. Staggering around the corner of the house, he encountered another machine gun nest with an unobstructed view of the quarry. That was it, of course, the fifty-nine bullets. When the barrage of slugs finally stopped, Aiello's black trench coat was like a sieve, and the wall of Prestogiacomo's house was a crumbling mess. Aiello had finally been outgunned and outgooned.

# GIUSEPPE "JOE THE BOSS" MASSERIA
## APRIL 15, 1931

### THE MAN WHO COULD DODGE BULLETS

Giuseppe Masseria had lofty ambitions. He wanted all the gangs of New York under his rule as *capo di tutti capi*—the Big Boss. His quest for the brass ring would plunge the city into a bloody battle that would never be forgotten and that ultimately cost him his life.

A lieutenant in the Morello Mob, Masseria challenged and defeated rival mobster Salvatore D'Aquila in the early 1920s. Though D'Aquila had tried to deal with Masseria in 1922, sending gunman Umberto Valenti to do the job, Masseria had miraculously survived all attempts made against his life. In fact, he had literally dodged Valenti's bullets, and the only casualty in the attack was his fedora hat. After this failed assassination, Masseria was considered bullet-proof.

Masseria now took control of Morello's old gang, with former boss Morello working under him, and leveraged his position. In 1928 D'Aquila himself was murdered, and with him pushing up the daisies, Masseria ran a healthy chunk of New York's underworld. Others may have referred to him as "the man who could dodge bullets", but Masseria referred to himself as the Boss of all Bosses.

In this role, Masseria put the muscle on the other mobs to

*Giuseppe 'Joe The Boss' Masseria*

fork over the tribute. But Salvatore Maranzano of the Castellammarese faction refused to pay up. In fact Maranzano had plans of his own and Masseria, with his demands for gold, was just mucking up the works. As the two vied for supremacy the bloodshed escalated. Soon New York was embroiled in what was to become one of the most significant battles within Mafia history—the Castellammarese War. It was a big one, and it changed everything.

## THE CASTELLAMMARESE WAR

One of the first casualties of the war was Masseria's old and respected boss Giuseppe Morello. But a Maranzano ally—Joe Aiello—was soon to follow. In fact, the hits went rapidly back and forth between the two sides until finally the Masseria faction began to crack. Masseria's men could see the writing on the wall and one by one they jumped ship. Masseria underling Lucky Luciano finally took the bull by the horns and decided it was time to put his boss out of his misery. Throwing his lot in with Maranzano, Luciano agreed to eliminate Masseria in return for gaining his operations and a seat at the big table within Maranzano's gang.

On April 15, 1931, Masseria met Luciano for lunch at the Nuova Villa Tammaro restaurant on Coney Island. After the luncheon, the two broke out a deck of cards and started to play. Some time during the course of the afternoon Luciano excused himself and got up. While he was gone, several men stepped through the doorway and shot Masseria as he shuffled the deck.

With the death of Masseria, Luciano hoped that a new age would be ushered in by Maranzano, and that the old, tradition-bound ways of the Mafia would be left behind. He was mistaken in this belief, however, and he was soon to conclude that the Castellammarese War was not quite over yet.

# SALVATORE MARANZANO
## SEPTEMBER 10, 1931

### LITTLE CAESAR

It was 1931. The Castellammarese War was over and the body of Joe "The Boss" Masseria was cooling in a morgue somewhere. Salvatore Maranzano took up his position as the new Boss—the *capo di tutti capi* of New York City.

Lucky Luciano had risked much to join Maranzano—he'd betrayed his old boss and put his backing behind an unknown. His hope was that Maranzano's victory would not only bring an end to a conflict that had lasted too long, but that Maranzano, unlike Masseria before him, would modernize the Mafia and its businesses.

At the time the mobs were overrun with what were known as "Moustache Petes"—old-world mafiosi who clung to dated and sometimes meaningless traditions. Hard-line Petes wouldn't do business with non-Italians. Some wouldn't even associate with non-Sicilians, and even then preferred only those from their own villages.

The Young Turks, as Luciano's generation was called, readily broke bread with other gangs, and incorporated different ethnic groups into their mobs. Nationality didn't enter into it. The Broadway Mob, to which Luciano belonged, included such names as Frank Costello and Joe Adonis to be sure, but also Bugsy Siegel and Meyer Lansky—heavy-hitters all of them. Old-fashioned notions only hindered the gangs' ability to make money.

### A NEW EMPEROR

Luciano, then, expected a lot from Maranzano. He had also been led to believe that the days of the overriding single Mafia boss had died with Masseria. But Maranzano had his own agenda, of course, and envisioned himself as the ruler of a new Roman Empire—a new Caesar. In fact the press called Sal "Little Caesar", like Edward G. Robinson in that 1931 flick of the same name. Maranzano inaugurated his new world order at a banquet held in late April of '31. During the celebration he rewarded his supporters, such as Luciano, dividing New York among them. But he also took the opportunity to assert his authority; like Masseria before him, Maranzano declared himself *capo di tutti capi*. This was not what Luciano had signed up for.

On September 10, 1931, Luciano sent over some hired guns to Maranzano's offices. These were non-mafiosi, men that Maranzano did not recognize—such was the price of his closed-mindedness. Posing as Internal Revenue agents, the gunmen had no trouble entering and were ushered in to see the Boss. Once inside, the killers quietly closed the door behind them and put an end to Little Caesar.

Once Maranzano was out of the way, Luciano abolished the position of *capo di tutti capi*, an institution that had caused far too much in-fighting. He also created the Commission—the ruling body that refereed the goings-on of the Mafia families—and the National Crime Syndicate, the agency that oversaw all under-world matters for every mob in the country. For the first time ever, crime was truly organized, and that meant power.

# THE COLLINGWOOD MANOR MASSACRE
## SEPTEMBER 16, 1931

## THE PURPLE GANG

The Purple Gang were the most notorious mob in Detroit during the Roaring Twenties. Chicago had the South Siders and the North Siders, as well as various bottom-feeders. New York was lousy with mobs, gangs who either learned to cooperate with each other or were demolished. But in Detroit it was the Purple Gang, and they had the city all sewn up.

Loosely controlled by four brothers—Abe, Joseph, Raymond and Isadore Bernstein—the gang had its fingers in all the money-making operations of the day: extortion, bootlegging, prostitution, narcotics, gambling, theft, hijacking, murder and of course abduction. They'd even been named as suspects in the kidnapping and murder of the baby son of aviation hero Charles Lindbergh. But then, so had half the underworld of the time.

As the Purple Gang grew in power, they began to get sloppy. But if an entire city has instant amnesia caused by the threat of a tommy gun, it's hard for the cops to make a case stick and with just about every public official on their payroll the Purples decided they could afford to let things slip a bit. After all, they thought, they were practically invincible. They were wrong.

## THE THIRD AVENUE TERRORS

Things began to fall apart for the Purples when Joseph Lebowitz, Isadore "Izzy the Rat" Sutker and Herman "Hymie" Paul came over from Chicago to avoid the ire of Al Capone. Once in the city, the three from Chicago joined up with a subgroup of the Purples called The Little Jewish Navy. They now dubbed themselves the Third Avenue Terrors and after a while they started to flex their muscles, disregarding territorial divisions and hijacking whisky shipments. The Terrors were trying to go into business for themselves.

In 1931 the Bernstein brothers decided it was time to put the Terrors in their place—permanently. On September 31, they called the three Terrors to a meeting at the Collingwood Manor apartments, supposedly to talk business. Everything seemed on the up and up. After all, the Terrors' buddy Sol Levine was even going to be there. What could go wrong?

The Terrors would soon find out. After the pleasantries had been exchanged and everyone was settled, the Purple Gang representatives—Harry Keywell, Irving Milberg and Harry Fleisher—drew their guns and opened fire on the three from Chicago, littering their bodies throughout the apartment. With their guns still smoking, the Purples exited the apartment and took off in a getaway car that Raymond Bernstein had been idling. And as far as the Purples were concerned that was that.

Except that by now Detroit had had enough and the authorities were under pressure to lower the boom. Three of the killers were soon rounded up—Bernstein, Keywell and Milberg. Fleisher was never caught. During the trial, Sol Levine—terrified of the Purples, but even more so of the police, apparently—put the finger on the gang and the defendants were sentenced to life in Marquette Prison. With three key members gone, the Purple Gang withered away and Detroit heaved a huge sigh of relief.

# JACK "LEGS" DIAMOND
## DECEMBER 18, 1931

### "AIN'T THERE NOBODY THAT CAN SHOOT THIS GUY SO HE DON'T BOUNCE BACK?"

Jack Moran, better known as "Legs" Diamond, was quite the hotshot in the Jazz Age. A Prohibition celebrity, Diamond was always in the papers or on the newsreels and that's just the way he liked it.

Jack Diamond embarked upon his criminal career in a small New York street gang, but in 1917 he was caught in the draft and did a short stint for Uncle Sam. Finding army life not to his liking, Diamond went AWOL—a little excursion that sent him to Leavenworth prison in Kansas for several years.

Once he was released, Diamond spent some time with Arnold Rothstein's mob before joining Little Augie Orgen's operation. But Diamond was less than successful in his role as Orgen's bodyguard. He was not able to save Orgen when the mobster's lieutenant, Louis Buchalter, came gunning for him in the fall of 1927. Orgen dropped like a stone that day, but Diamond was merely wounded. It would be only one of many attempts on Diamond's life—five in total—all of which earned Diamond the nickname of the Clay Pigeon.

Whether or not Diamond had anything to do with Orgen's demise is unknown. He certainly profited from the gangster's downfall, though, when Buchalter gave him a slice of Orgen's old operations.

## THE HOTSY TOTSY CLUB

Diamond now cut out on his own, running bootlegging and drug rackets. He opened a night spot, the Hotsy Totsy Club, and it was at this time that he became known as a flamboyant man about town. His new girlfriend, Kiki Roberts, was a Ziegfeld girl, no less. But Diamond was soon in competition with rival mobster Dutch Schultz and the two became bitter enemies. After yet another failed attempt had been made on Diamond's life, it was Dutch who moaned "Ain't there nobody who can shoot this guy so he don't bounce back?" Apparently, not yet.

After a trip to Europe, ostensibly to recover from the latest attempt on his life but also to scout out alcohol and drug suppliers, Diamond endured several more attempted assassinations while he struggled to renew his operations. But time was running out for Legs Diamond.

The end came while he was temporarily residing in Albany, New York. Diamond was in town successfully defending himself against a kidnapping rap and had flopped at a boarding house. Just before dawn on the morning of December 18, 1931, Diamond, who had been celebrating his acquittal, returned to his room tipsy and exhausted and threw himself onto the bed. A short while later two men broke into the room and as one of them held Diamond down, the other shot him three times in the head. He wasn't able to get up from this one.

The killers of Legs Diamond have never been identified. Suspicion has fallen on Dutch Schultz, who certainly gets points for trying, but it has also been speculated that Diamond's murderers were actually members of the Albany police force. The police in Albany had crime in that town all sewn up. Fearing that Diamond would move in on their rackets, the cops may well have shown up that morning in December to take Diamond out of the competition.

# VINCENT COLL
## FEBRUARY 8, 1932

### "MAD DOG" COLL

Vincent "Mad Dog" Coll worked for a while in Dutch Schultz's mob during the 1920s. Schultz found Coll a useful enforcer—he seemed to have little conscience and plenty of gall, a combination that Schultz found advantageous, at least for a while.

But Coll was a loose cannon, to say the least. He earned the nickname "Mad Dog" from the accidental shooting to death of a young child, five-year-old Michael Vengalli. Coll had been trying to get mobster Joseph Rao, but when he sprayed the street with bullets in one of those epic shoot-outs of the time, several small children were hit in the barrage and little Michael was killed. After that incident, police officials considered Coll something less than human—a mad dog.

Coll would often improvise while carrying out jobs for Schultz, a trait his boss did not appreciate. On one occasion, going beyond his orders, Coll killed speakeasy-owner Anthony Borello because he refused to carry Schultz's hooch. Another time, again without Schultz's authorization, Coll robbed a dairy, helping himself to the hefty cashbox. Schultz was furious at all the unwanted heat these activities brought. But Coll thought he was worth it. In fact he thought he was worth much more and when confronted about his faux pas, his reaction was to demand Schultz take him on as partner in his mob. The Dutchman, not very politely, refused.

Coll now struck out on his own, the animosity between himself and Schultz building to epic proportions. As an entrepreneur, Coll fell back on that tried and trusted money-making scheme of kidnapping mob bosses for profit—a risky prospect to say the least, but Coll reasoned his plan had to pay off, at least in the short term. The gangs would be unable to call the police for help—for obvious reasons—and they'd have to cough up. But inevitably Mad Dog was antagonizing some very powerful figures in New York's underworld.

One such figure was Hell's Kitchen boss Owney Madden. Coll angered Madden by pulling his kidnapping racket on Madden's friend, gangster George DeMange. DeMange was released after the ransom was paid, but Coll may as well have painted a big red target on himself.

### ONE KIDNAPPING TOO MANY

Inevitably, Coll tried his kidnapping gag once too often. In 1932, apparently trying to put the squeeze on Madden once again, he contacted him from a public telephone in the London Chemists drugstore on West 23rd Street. As Coll stood in the booth, a car pulled up and three men got out. Stepping into the store, the men opened fire on Coll, filling him full of lead. Coll, hit at least fifteen times, collapsed in the booth. The Mad Dog had been put down.

Coll's killers were never identified, but both Dutch Schultz and Owney Madden had one less enemy. By the end of that day in February the man who dared to prey on the mobsters was gone.

# CHARLES "VANNIE" HIGGINS
## JUNE 19, 1932

### THE AVIATOR

No doubt on certain nights during the late 1920s and early 1930s the plane of Charles "Vannie" Higgins could be seen on its way from Canada to the United States. Higgins used to run rum with his plane. He used other methods of transport too, of course, including trucks, taxis and boats, his famous vessel *The Cigarette* being just one of them. But it was the plane he loved and he would often fly it himself.

Higgins had cut his criminal teeth in "Big Bill" Dwyer's gang in the 1920s and when he struck out on his own he came into conflict with Dutch Schultz during the bootlegging wars of Manhattan. Everybody seemed to bump shoulders with Schultz. Higgins apparently sided with "Legs" Diamond and Vincent Coll against Schultz and the streets would regularly erupt with their gun battles.

Higgins had numerous run-ins with the law and was arrested any number of times. He was only convicted once, however, and that conviction resulted in a fine rather than jail time. It seems that whenever Higgins went to trial witnesses would go missing, or find that they suddenly had to leave on some spurious excuse. Higgins, of course, also had a number of highly placed friends who always came through in a scrape.

Shortly before Higgins was killed he flew his plane to New

York's Great Meadow Maximum Correctional Facility for a visit with his old pal the warden. Warden Wilson had conscripted the prisoners to clear a landing field for Higgins and the two spent the day reminiscing, no doubt with the lifers milling about just yards away. New York Governor Franklin Delano Roosevelt didn't care for Warden Wilson fraternizing with the likes of Higgins, a known gangster, but the warden let it roll off his back—his friends were his own business, he told the future president.

## VALIANT VANNIE

But Vannie Higgins's overriding concern was his family, and shortly after his visit with Warden Wilson he was compelled to make the ultimate sacrifice for them. On the night of June 19, 1932, Higgins attended a recital of his seven-year-old daughter's dance class surrounded by family members, along with some enforcers, of course.

As Higgins and company were leaving the building after the performance, a car pulled up on the darkened street. Several men carrying guns stepped out and began shooting. Acting fast, Higgins pushed his family aside and ran down the street, drawing the fire of the gunmen. After collapsing on the ground, he was taken to the nearest hospital. He held on for about fifteen hours, enduring several blood transfusions, but really his death was a foregone conclusion. Refusing to name his assailants, Higgins died, still swearing he would get his killers.

Though Higgins may have known who killed him, his murderers were never actually identified—but when Brooklyn D.A. William O'Dwyer began proceedings against Murder Incorporated in 1940, Higgins was named as just one of the many targets of that organization. Higgins may have lived a gangster, but in the end, it could be argued, he died a hero.

# CHARLES "KING" SOLOMON
## JANUARY 24, 1933

### NIGHTS AT THE COCOANUT GROVE

Charles Solomon—colourfully known as "King" Solomon—was the pre-eminent bootlegger in Boston during the 1920s. Of course, he had other interests as well—narcotics, gambling, pandering. But for Solomon, the demon rum was king, and he used his fleet of ships to bring in liquor from Central American and Canada. Solomon sold prime stuff then, not the homemade rotgut that some bootleggers would foist on their hapless customers. And for "King" Solomon, court was his nightclub, the Cocoanut Grove, one of the most popular spots in Boston.

Solomon owned the Grove from 1927 until his death in 1933, and it was a classy joint. Decorated in a South Sea island theme, the Grove featured swaying palm trees and a roof that would slide back in order to enhance the atmosphere. Many's the time the King could be found there, surrounded by celebrities and taking care of mob business. After leaving the Grove, Solomon would do the rounds of Boston's other hot spots, such as the Cotton Club.

### *THE ATLANTIC CITY CONFERENCE*

As a major power in Massachusetts, Solomon was a Boston representative at the Atlantic City Conference that took place in 1929. The Conference was an early mob summit and anyone who was anyone in gangland was there. The get-together was hardly clandestine, and throughout the festivities the press was on hand to snap shots of Enoch "Nucky" Johnson, Meyer Lansky, Dutch Schultz and Charlie Luciano. But though there was plenty of entertainment at the Conference, it was not all play and no work. The meeting represented the first large step toward the real organization of crime and paved the way for the creation of the National Crime Syndicate.

Unfortunately the spirit of cooperation, peace and brotherly love that the Conference tried to engender did not translate to Boston itself. During the late 1920s and early 1930s, several rival groups contended for supremacy in the city. Making a lot of noise was Philip Buccola, boss of what would later become Boston's powerful Patriarca family. Buccola (a gangster who lived to be 101) had his enforcers and wise guys making the rounds, wiping out the competition as they went. As the Buccola goons made their way to the Cocoanut Grove and Solomon's seat of power, the King's days as top dog were numbered.

The hit came in the early morning of January 28, 1933, after Solomon had left the Grove and headed to the Cotton Club to dance away the wee hours. In attendance were a couple of chorus girls whom Solomon was entertaining for the evening. At some time during the celebrations, Solomon excused himself and headed to the men's room. So did two broken-nose types and during the scuffle, which could be heard on the dance floor, Solomon received several slugs in the chest and neck. That was the end of Charles Solomon.

No one registered any astonishment when Buccola advanced his position in the city and became the rising star in Boston. The king was dead, long live the king.

*A mugshot of Gus Winkler, courtesy of the Chicago Police department.*

# GUS WINKLER
## OCTOBER 9, 1933

### THE AMERICAN BOYS

Gus Winkler was a safe-cracker, torpedo and freelance hood during the days of Prohibition. The highlight of Winkler's criminal career was undoubtedly becoming a pal of Al "Scarface" Capone. Though Gus was considered a gutless wonder, he'd somehow made it into Capone's good books and was used by the mob boss for special cases, including the assassination of Frankie Yale and that hit of all hits, the St. Valentine's Day Massacre.

Starting out in the St. Louis gang Egan's Rats, Winkler hooked up with Fred "Killer" Burke and Bob Carey. When things fell apart for the Rats in 1924, Winkler ended up in Chicago, by way of Detroit. It was some time during this period that he lost an eye during a mail robbery. A vain man, Winkler hoped to polish his image and took to wearing glasses in order to camouflage the disfigurement.

Winkler, Burke and Carey came to the attention of Al Capone at this time, doing some priority jobs for him, most notably that big one in 1929. Capone referred to them as "The American Boys". But the gang were enterprising and pulled numerous heists on their own, holding up armoured cars and robbing banks in New Jersey, Wisconsin, Los Angeles and Ohio. Revenue from these robberies would allow Winkler to act as something of a gangland broker for criminal enterprises and to open an underworld safe-house for mobsters on the run.

Winkler was described as self-obsessed and somewhat talkative, and it was undoubtedly this chatty quality that would later get him into trouble. The end came for him on October 9, 1933, when he was shot down on Roscoe Street. Though, as in the case of so many others, Winkler's killers were never identified, the truth is that the assassins could have been just about anyone in the syndicate. Winkler, trusted by no one, had made it perfectly clear on more than one occasion that he was out for himself no matter what. Though he'd apparently enjoyed a certain amount of protection from Capone, once Scarface was sent up the river, the new boss of the Chicago Outfit—Frank Nitti—had no use for Winkler.

Suspicion about the death has also fallen on Roger Touhy and his Chicago gang. In December 1932, Winkler participated with the Touhy mob in a mail robbery worth $250,000. Winkler himself had worried that the gang was after him because he hadn't divided the loot to their liking.

### DANGEROUS MEMOIRS

In any case, on that day in October, Winkler went down and he went down hard—a total of seventy-two bullets and buckshot pellets had passed through his body, ensuring that he would never get up again. And Winkler's link to the St. Valentine's Day Massacre? It was his wife, Georgette, who later revealed his connection with that epic slaughter. During Winkler's criminal career the blonde and beautiful Georgette had acted as his right hand, often vetting his contracts. After his death, Georgette attempted to publish her memoirs—a work that outlined her husband's relationship to the mob. But the piece was considered too hot at the time and remained unpublished until its discovery several years ago, when it blew the lid off the massacre.

# VERNON CLATE MILLER
## NOVEMBER 29, 1933

### FROM HERO TO OUTLAW

There are legendary figures of the Roaring Twenties and Dirty Thirties, gangsters who spring to mind in the context of bold bank robberies, bullet-riddled cars and smoking machine guns. Pretty Boy Floyd, Bonnie and Clyde, Machine Gun Kelly—they personify the period. But there's one of this crowd, one of the bloody and lawless, who today is apparently remembered only by a few—Vernon Clate Miller. Back in the day, though, Miller was a force to be reckoned with.

So, who was Vernon Miller? You wouldn't know it from the way he died—he'd been trussed up and dumped on a dirt road—but at one time, he was a highly respected individual. A member of the National Guard who had fought Mexican rebel Pancho Villa, Miller also did his bit "over there" and came back as a decorated war hero, lionized for his bravery. Once Stateside again, Miller took up the position of Sheriff in his home of Huron, South Dakota and was known as tough but honest.

And then things suddenly veered off in an entirely different direction. Maybe it was shell shock from the Great War, or maybe Miller was suffering from an advanced case of syphilis as one source indicates (though there is no further verification on that, so it may just be embellishment). If so, either one of these conditions could have caused Miller's mind to rapidly deteriorate.

In any case, one fine day in August of 1922 Miller embezzled $6000 from the treasury of Beadle County, North Dakota, and skipped town. After that, it was all downhill for Vernon Clate Miller.

To start the criminal ball rolling, Miller dabbled in bootlegging like everybody else at that time; and then he got into gambling, making friends with Louis Buchalter. But as with the other Desperados—Floyd, the Barkers, Parker and Barrow—it was bank robbery that really gave Miller a sense of purpose. And as his criminal career progressed, he became more and more unpredictable; something was certainly amiss in the mind of Vernon Miller.

Between 1927 and early 1933, Miller took part in no fewer than eight bank robberies. He and his gang were responsible for at least twenty-seven gunshot deaths or injuries—a number of these members of Miller's own mob, of course. In the Kansas City Massacre alone, when Miller's gang tried to free bank robber Frank Nash from law enforcement officers, five were killed. By now, Miller had become one of the FBI's most wanted, and the cross-country manhunt was on.

### DEATH IN KANSAS CITY

But the Feds were not the only ones after Miller. The Kansas City Massacre was something of a disaster, and as a result the underworld was now experiencing a lot of heat. The most logical solution, as far as the mobs were concerned (and that included Buchalter of Murder Incorporated) was to remove the focal point of all this attention.

And that's how Vernon Clate Miller, legendary gangster and public enemy, ended up dead on a dirt road on November 29, 1933. When the autopsy was performed on the pulpy residue that Miller had become, it became evident that he had been tortured, then strangled. No doubt he would have much preferred to go out in a blaze of bullets in Thirties style.

The fatal shooting of Frank Nash and his police escort in front of Union Railway Station, Kansas City, 1933.

# JOHN LAZIA
## JULY 10, 1934

### THE KANSAS CITY MASSACRE

It is largely forgotten these days, but in 1933 the Kansas City Massacre caused quite a ruckus. And when it was all over, and four officers plus their prisoner lay dead, mob boss John Lazia really should have known that his time was nearly up too.

Lazia, together with prominent politician Tom Pendergast, ruled Kansas City in the early 1930s. Pendergast took care of the official aspect, greasing wheels and making sure that the right people (and that meant Pendergast people) held the right jobs. Lazia and his underboss Charles Carrollo, meanwhile, oversaw the more colourful angles. Pendergast, of course, got his fair share of all the rackets.

It's said that Kansas was the best-run corrupt city in the country, due in no small way to Lazia. As part of his understanding with Pendergast, Lazia kept a lid on violent crime, while Pendergast turned a blind eye to the less "serious" (and more profitable) crimes of bootlegging and gambling. From his desk at the police station (no less), Lazia kept tabs on all illegal activity in Kansas City: no crook could enter the city without his say-so, and no crime could be committed without his okay—or else. For a while, the system worked exceedingly well.

This state of affairs changed in early 1933, however, when the Lazia regime sustained several dents to its prestige. That year saw the kidnapping of an important heiress (not a Lazia-approved crime), plus the rise of several local hoods who had begun to muscle their way into the mobster's territory.

### SHOOT-OUT AT UNION STATION

But things really spun out of control with the Kansas City Massacre in June of 1933. Bank-robber Frank Nash was going to be transferred to Leavenworth prison after years on the run. Several of Nash's friends decided they wanted to spring the convict and planned to hijack the convoy as it arrived at Union Station.

The group approached Lazia for approval, just as they should, and the mobster gave them the thumbs up. He also supplied them, it's said, with additional gunmen—apparently Adam Richetti and "Pretty Boy" Floyd among them! Pretty Boy Floyd—now there's a name from criminal legend. It's now thought that Richetti and Floyd did not actually take part in this particular adventure, but it makes for a great story.

What happened next was absolute chaos. By the end of the hijacking four officers were dead, and so was Nash. But then, maybe Nash had been a target all along.

After the massacre, though, Kansas City was agog and Pendergast found it expeditious to distance himself from Lazia. When the mob boss was indicted on tax evasion charges in 1934, Pendergast was nowhere to be found and Lazia was sentenced to a year in jail. What's more, Pendergast now began to put his support behind another gang. The writing for Lazia was on the wall.

On July 10, 1934, Lazia was shot down while returning to his lavish apartment after a night on the town with his wife and his bodyguard. The coroner later reported that the gangster had been killed by one of the guns that had been used in the massacre—an inside job. It was no shock to anybody then when Charles Carrollo, Lazia's second in command, became the next big thing in Kansas City.

# FERDINAND BOCCIA
## SEPTEMBER, 1934

### JUSTICE FOR "THE SHADOW"

The hit on Ferdinand Boccia haunted mobster Vito Genovese for decades. It seemed that Boccia just couldn't stay buried and kept popping up at the most inconvenient times, forcing the gangster to relocate twice and delaying his elevation to crime boss by two decades. Evidently "The Shadow", as Boccia was known, had a score to settle.

Genovese and Boccia were members of the Luciano mob in the mid 1930s. The pair came up with the notion of bilking a visiting Italian out of a small fortune in a crooked card game. Boccia introduced Genovese to the mark and during the course of the game the gangsters managed to relieve the gentleman of a cool hundred and fifty grand. The only problem was that when it came to dividing the money, Boccia, as the man who had supplied the victim, thought that he was worth more than the amount Genovese had allotted him. This was a big mistake on his part.

Some time in 1934, possibly September 19, Genovese had Boccia shot as he sat enjoying a cappuccino in a Brooklyn coffee shop. The killers were probably Cosmo "Gus" Frasca and George Smurra. The two killers then dumped Boccia's body into the Hudson River, where it bobbed quietly for three years.

In the meantime, in 1936, mob boss Lucky Luciano was

sentenced to fifty years in prison, and while he was gone Genovese managed to take up the mantle of godfather for the Luciano mob. But his first tenure as boss was to be short-lived. Apparently a body had just been discovered floating in the Hudson and now there was this small matter of murder to be dealt with— Boccia had returned. Not waiting around to be arrested, Genovese caught the next boat to Naples.

Things weren't too bad at first for the gangster in Italy. He was able to settle into a comfortable life as a racketeer operating in Sicily and incidentally doing small jobs for Mussolini. When the Allies entered the country in 1943, Genovese easily switched uniforms, as it were, and acted as interpreter and liaison for the American army. But concurrent to this role, Genovese was also helping himself to military supplies and selling them on the black market.

## BACK TO THE USA

Finally, one enterprising CID Agent, O.C. Dickey, did some digging on Genovese and linked him to an outstanding homicide back in the States. Seems there was once this mobster called Ferdinand Boccia . . . Once more Genovese was compelled to board ship, this time going back to New York to face charges for the murder of his former collaborator.

Although the charges against Genovese for the murder of Boccia were eventually dropped, he received no real backing from his old mob upon his return to the United States. He took over a small gang in Greenwich Village, and it would be another eleven years before he was able to rise to the position of boss of the entire Genovese family. But his years as boss were nothing if not turbulent—it was he who arranged the ill-fated Apalachin Meeting, the event that allowed the police to finally get some firm evidence on the existence of the mob. In revenge for this debacle the Commission framed Genovese on a narcotics charge. Genovese was sent up for fifteen years and he died in prison. Was it final justice for The Shadow? Well, for him, and for scores of others.

# LOUIS ALTERIE
## JULY 18, 1935

### "TWO-GUN" ALTERIE

One of the slickest moves to come out of the Roaring Twenties was the "ambush murder". In this type of hit, snipers would rent a location across the street from a joint their victim was known to frequent. Then, when the mark showed up, the assassins would lay waste to him in a spray of bullets. The technique was precise and methodical, one that was sure to guarantee success. And it was a method of murder made famous by Louis "Two-Gun" Alterie.

Louis Alterie was a member of Dean O'Banion's North Side gang. Though he lived and worked throughout the twenties in Chicago, Alterie's heart—he always said—was in the West, where he loved to put his feet up at his ranch. The descendant of Spanish and French ranchers in California, Alterie saw himself as a cowboy and tended to dress the part. Tall, with dark slicked-back hair, he must have cut quite a figure when he was all duded up in his ten-gallon hat, cowboy boots and diamond-studded belt, especially when standing next to some torpedo from New York looking all slick in pinstripes and a fedora.

Alterie also loved to let loose like an outlaw in a saloon. Case in point: when Dean O'Banion was killed, Alterie told all and sundry, including the press, that he wanted to meet the killers out in the street somewhere and shoot it out, Western style.

After this outburst the rest of the North Siders convinced Alterie to retire for a while—they had enough on their hands with Al Capone and didn't need any extra scrutiny from the press and the police.

## AMBUSHED BY THE CHICAGO OUTFIT

Alterie laid low for a while on his ranch then, punching cows and lassoing longhorns. But Two-Gun being Two-Gun, it didn't take long before he got into an altercation or two. Shooting up the Denver Hotel, Alterie was arrested and after his conviction was banished from Colorado for a period of five years.

So Alterie headed back to Chicago. It was now 1933, and America was knee-deep in the Depression. Though the North Siders were still limping along, their power had been greatly depleted. Despite this, Alterie was able to slip easily once more into the life of a racketeer, making a tidy sum in the labour unions. But Alterie hadn't counted on the Chicago Outfit. Though Capone was in jail, his mob had the city all sewn up and they weren't looking to share their labour profits with Alterie.

On July 18, 1935, as Alterie and his wife were leaving their hotel, shots rang out from across the street. Alterie spun around, arms in the air, then fell to the ground, hit by a total of nine bullets. He died later that day on the operating table, a victim of an ambush, the very technique he had pioneered. Louis "Two-Gun" Alterie had gone to that big ranch in the sky.

# ABRAHAM "BO" WEINBERG
## SEPTEMBER 9, 1935

### WEINBERG SLEEPS WITH THE FISHES

Abraham "Bo" Weinberg was a lieutenant in Dutch Schultz's mob. For a long time he was Schultz's right-hand man and his most trusted enforcer. But Schultz was an erratic soul, and as his underworld power grew, so did his eccentricities. In 1933 he was indicted for tax evasion. This was the same thing that had spelled "finis" for the mighty Capone and Schultz decided it was high time for him to take a little vacation. For a while then he went on the lam and Weinberg ran the Schultz mob in his absence.

Weinberg had done a number of extremely delicate pieces of work for Schultz, allegedly including the assassinations of Legs Diamond, Mad Dog Coll and, one theory suggests, Arnold "The Brain" Rothstein. But in taking control of the Schultz gang, Weinberg's concerns began to grow. Schultz was an expensive commodity. On the lam he'd been racking up bills, and when he finally came out of hiding to face the music in 1934, his legal fees were eating up profits.

So Weinberg approached the National Crime Syndicate—the underworld ruling body—and offered to cut a deal with them. He feared that Schultz's gang would soon unravel and that Charlie "Lucky" Luciano and the Syndicate would divvy up the remains of the Dutchman's enterprises anyway, so why not meet them in the middle? Maybe this way Weinberg could still retain control over the majority of the mob's operations. Luciano felt slightly differently about things, though, and began to make moves to distribute Schultz's regime among the members of the Syndicate.

### THE DUTCHMAN GOES FREE

Imagine everyone's surprise, then, when in 1935 Schultz was back, his trials ending in acquittal. By acting like a good citizen—donating bags of toys to orphans, giving money to charity and in general kissing babies—the Dutchman had managed to sway the jury, much to the astonishment of the judge.

Schultz was astonished too when he came back to his empire and found things significantly altered. Not to worry, Luciano explained, they'd only been minding house while Schultz was otherwise occupied, and now things could revert to normal. The idiosyncratic Schultz reportedly teared up when he heard Luciano's side of things, but Luciano knew there was more going on with Schultz than met the eye.

The Dutchman now had a major score to settle with Weinberg. No points for guessing what happened next. One night, after leaving a Manhattan nightspot, Weinberg disappeared and was never seen again. A story exists—and they always do—that it was Schultz himself who put a bullet into Weinberg's head that night. In any case, it's widely believed that Schultz had Weinberg encased in cement—either totally or just his feet—and then dumped into the river. As his body has never been recovered, it can probably be said with accuracy that Bo Weinberg sleeps with the fishes.

# LOUIS "PRETTY" AMBERG
## OCTOBER 23, 1935

### MURDER INCORPORATED

Truly one of the most hated gangsters in New York, there was actually nothing attractive at all about Pretty Amberg. Nature had given him a rather unfortunate appearance, to put it mildly, but Amberg could not have cared less about his looks. Supposedly once offered a job in a circus as the missing link, Amberg, far from being offended by this, claimed bragging rights on the offer.

Amberg was a loan shark and bootlegger and ran some rackets in Brooklyn with his brothers Joseph and Hyman. He liked things on the tough side and would reputedly spit into diners' soup bowls as he entered a restaurant. He also had a nasty habit of killing transients on the street. Once sarcastically described by author Damon Runyon as being in the laundry business, Amberg would stuff his victims into a bag and tie them up with wire in such a way that they would strangle themselves as they struggled. For a while the Brownsville section of Brooklyn was littered with laundry bag corpses. All in all, Pretty Amberg was a pretty gruesome customer.

The Ambergs' rackets stayed modest for only a while and as the brothers began to rake in the money, interest from the other mobsters grew, including such heavyweights as Owney Madden and Legs Diamond. Dutch Schultz took quite a fancy to the

Amberg operation and once commented to Amberg that it might be a good idea if they went into business together. Amberg was less than enthusiastic about this idea, to say the least. Actually Amberg suggested that Schultz take his own gun and shoot himself with it.

### BUCHALTER AND SHAPIRO

But the Ambergs were also drawing into competition with Louis "Lepke" Buchalter and Jacob "Gurrah" Shapiro for what was becoming increasingly valuable territory. Madden, Diamond and Schultz (especially Schultz) were dangerous enough, but when the Ambergs started locking horns with Louis Buchalter, they were also locking horns with the Syndicate's assassination arm— Murder Incorporated.

The Amberg gang began to disintegrate pretty rapidly after that. Brother Hyman had already died in 1926, killing himself after a failed prison escape attempt. Joseph and Louis were still around—though it must be said, they weren't around for long. In September of 1935 Joseph and his bodyguard/chauffeur Morris Kessler were killed in what was to be one of the first major jobs for the murder organization. They were gunned down while collecting protection money from a Brooklyn auto repair shop.

Pretty Amberg was soon to follow. In fact less than a month later, on October 23, 1935, he met his demise. His body had been bound with wire and set ablaze inside a car. As it turned out that week in October was a busy one for Murder Incorporated. Buchalter and his buddies also rubbed out the legendary mobster Dutch Schultz the very next day.

# DUTCH SCHULTZ
## OCTOBER 24, 1935

### THE DUTCHMAN

His real name was Arthur Flegenheimer, but he preferred to be called Dutch—Dutch Schultz. As a bootlegger, gangster and racketeer during the late 1920s through the mid 1930s, Schultz was one of the big ones, right up there with Lucky Luciano, Bugsy Siegel and Al Capone. His was a name embedded in mob lore and one to be reckoned with.

Fearless, ambitious and intelligent, Schultz was a unique individual, to say the least. Heck, half the underworld thought that he was nuts. Charming and affable one minute, Schultz could erupt with a violent temper the next. He could also kill a man as coolly as he lit a cigarette. Any up-and-comer who dared lock horns with the Dutchman soon thought better of it, if they could still think at all. Schultz battled with the likes of Mad Dog Coll and Legs Diamond and came out on top.

But Schultz hadn't reckoned on the zeal of special prosecutor Thomas Dewey, who had a mission—get rid of mobsters like Schultz no matter what the personal risk.

In 1935 Schultz was tried twice for tax evasion. Putting his vast fortune into his court battles, he launched a huge goodwill campaign that made him seem like a kind-hearted citizen wrongly placed on the hot seat. Schultz was ultimately triumphant in court and his second trial ended in acquittal. But Dewey wasn't done

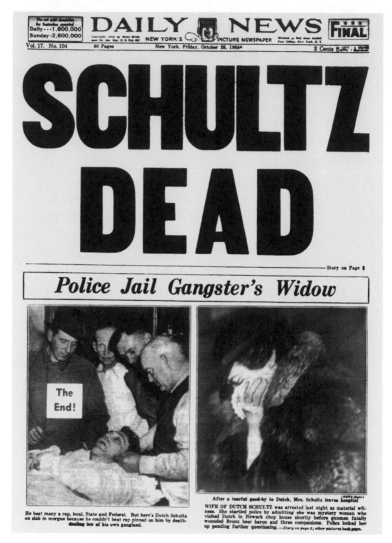

Daily News *front page, 25th of October, 1935, reporting the fatal shooting of Dutch Schultz; and the arrest of the gangster's widow.*

yet and he began to build a case against the Dutchman that was rumoured to include accusations of racketeering and murder. If convicted of this last item Schultz could go to the electric chair.

Schultz brought his grievance to the National Crime Syndicate—Luciano, Siegel, Louis Buchalter, et al. He had a job for Murder Incorporated, he said—he wanted them to take care of Dewey for him and he was willing to pay whatever it took.

### CONTRACT ON DEWEY

Unquestionably this request caused some raised eyebrows among the members of the Syndicate. Well, actually, they mostly thought Schultz had lost his marbles. Eliminating someone of Dewey's standing would categorically bring a reprisal that none in the underworld would survive.

No, Dewey wouldn't be rubbed out. Instead Luciano had a better idea and he put it to a vote—after Schultz had left the room, of course.

On October 24, 1935, as Schultz was dining at the Palace Chop House in New Jersey, several gunmen entered. He was in the rest room when the killers opened fire. Shot in the gut, he managed to stagger to a table where he collapsed into a chair. At first it seemed that his chances were good, but after the bullet had been removed, infection set in (the bullets had been treated with rust, an old mob trick) and Schultz spent the next twenty-two hours in agonized delirium, muttering incoherently. With ravings such as "don't let Satan draw you too fast", Schultz's deathbed ramblings have become entrenched in his legend, and read like psychedelic poetry.

But in all his ramblings Schultz made no mention of who shot him—they never do.

# "MACHINE GUN" JACK MCGURN
## FEBRUARY 15, 1936

### ARCHITECT OF THE MASSACRE

Jack McGurn was Al Capone's top bodyguard, and one of his chief enforcers. Nicknamed "Machine Gun" because of his use of the Thompson submachine gun during jobs, McGurn's real name was Vincenzo Antonio Gibaldi; and it was Gibaldi, reputedly, who was the brain behind the St. Valentine's Day Massacre.

McGurn had started out as a professional boxer, but with one thing and another, he gravitated to the Capone franchise mob, the Circus Gang. With his cool professionalism and willingness to pull the trigger, McGurn was quick to catch the attention of Capone, who welcomed him into his inner circle. McGurn proved invaluable to Capone and uncovered several assassination plots against the mobster's life, heading off would-be killers before they could pull the trigger.

McGurn was part-owner of a speakeasy—the Green Mill Jazz Club—and there's a story about how he dealt with a performer who wanted to work for another joint. Comedian and singer Joe E. Lewis was offered a better deal at another club and decided it was time to pick up stakes. McGurn suggested Lewis should think again. But Lewis went anyway and McGurn sent over some thugs to have a little talk with the comedian. Though the mobsters slit Lewis' throat and removed part of his tongue, Lewis miraculously survived. It would be several years, however, before he was able to speak or entertain again.

## THE BLONDE ALIBI

This gruesome incident aside, McGurn's greatest claim to fame was as the architect of the St. Valentine's Day Massacre. Probably one of the triggermen in the legendary hit, McGurn was charged with seven counts of murder, but was able to beat the rap. He'd spent the entire day with his girlfriend, Louise Rolfe, or so he said. Rolfe's corroborating statement got McGurn off the hook and ever after that she was known as McGurn's Blonde Alibi.

After Capone went to prison, though, McGurn's clout began to diminish. Named Public Enemy Number Four in 1930, he was becoming a risky commodity. The Outfit's new boss, Frank Nitti, found it advisable to distance the gang from McGurn, who was drawing too much attention to the mob. Nitti didn't like McGurn anyway.

With no underworld assignments to support him, McGurn turned to professional golf for a while, but his days were numbered. There's really no such thing as a retired gangster, and he had started to hit the bottle pretty hard. Who could tell what valuable information he might give away?

On February 15, 1936, McGurn was gunned down while spending the day bowling at the Avenue Recreation Bowling Alley. A Valentine card had been left in McGurn's name at the front desk of the alley. Because of this card there has been some speculation that the murder was in retaliation for the St. Valentine's Day Massacre, a hit that went down exactly seven years and one day before Jack's death. It's more likely, however, that Frank Nitti had McGurn rubbed out to keep him from talking and the Valentine's card was just colourful camouflage.

The body of Walter Sage discovered in Swan Lake in the Catskills, 31st of July 1937.

# WALTER SAGE
## 1937

### MURDER INC. AND THE MOVIES

Jack Gordon was a star in New York; he was also a star in L.A. Lighting up the silver screen in such second-feature flicks as *Jungle Raiders* and *Gambler's Choice*, Gordon worked as a bit actor and extra in Hollywood. But Gordon wasn't really an actor (a viewing of any one of his performances might confirm that). No, Jack Gordon was actually Irving "Big Gangi" Cohen, a low-level hood who at one time had worked for Walter Sage out in the Catskills.

Both Sage and Cohen were occasional hired killers, but mainly made their living by picking up money from slot machines and dropping it off to the mob. The only problem was that Sage developed sticky fingers and started skimming a little money off the top. That's when a contract was put out on Walter and three gunmen from Murder Incorporated—Abe Levine, Jack Drucker and Pittsburgh Phil—were sent over some time in 1937 to take care of the situation. The killers conscripted Sage's buddy Cohen to help them. That way, when they took Sage out for a little ride, he wouldn't expect a thing.

The day arrived and Drucker and Cohen went off with Sage in a car; Phil and Levine followed behind. As they were driving, Cohen suddenly reached forward and held Sage down as Drucker proceeded to stab him with an ice pick. Some reports indicate that Drucker also got a little over-zealous and accidentally stabbed Cohen in the arm too; but the job was done and Sage was very, very dead.

### *RUN FOR YOUR LIFE*

Now they had to get rid of the body. The plan was to weigh Sage down with a slot machine in an ironic gesture and toss him into deep water. As soon as the car stopped moving, though, Cohen leapt from the back seat and ran off screaming into the woods. He was either appalled by what he had done or thought that he too was a target. Maybe it was a little of both. Where Cohen went nobody knew and as long as he stayed quiet, no one was likely to come after him so they let him run.

So it was a surprise in 1939 when Levine, attending a matinée performance of a new boxing flick, *Golden Boy*, happened to catch a glimpse of Cohen in a crowd scene. He squinted, looked twice. Yes, it was Cohen all right. It seems that Cohen had made a beeline for Hollywood, where he had managed to find work as an extra.

So much for lying low. Now everyone knew where Cohen was, and the body of Sage had been found in Swan Lake in the Catskills in July 1937. Abe Levine, who had decided to turn informer, started to name names in a big way and implicated Cohen in the killing of Sage. Cohen was picked up by the police.

Cohen went to trial for the murder of Sage but gave such an emotional and convincing performance (probably his best) that the jury acquitted him. He was a free man and returned to Hollywood to further his career by appearing in such B flicks as *Prison Train*, though he does have a small part as a gangster in *Some Like it Hot*. That must have been typecasting.

# PETER PANTO
## JULY 14, 1939

### WHERE IS PETER PANTO?

"Where is Peter Panto?" The cry went up through the docks. It had been a mob killing, for sure, since most disappearances on the docks had to do with the mob. The shipping companies, the unions, the foremen—they were all mobbed-up, no question. It was precisely this that Panto was fighting against—corruption on the piers and in the unions, the lack of security, the abysmal and dangerous working conditions. But at that time, if you took a stand on the waterfront, you were butting heads with Albert Anastasia and Murder Incorporated. Needless to say, you didn't stand very long.

No doubt about it, shipping offered an unquestionable fortune to the mob at that time. Not only did the mob control the unions, demanding payment from workers just for the privilege of working, but they muscled the shipping companies as well, using the threat of strikes to get what they wanted. The Mafia could freely help itself to cargo that the ships brought in, literally lifting whole boatloads of goods and bringing in contraband from all over the world.

Peter Panto was an Italian immigrant, a dockworker trying to make an honest living through the back-breaking and irregular work on the piers. Peter was also an activist, a voice for workers' rights who had started a rank and file movement to improve working conditions, and to challenge the mob. Because the two of course went hand in hand; nothing could ever improve on the piers while the mob was around.

### THE FIRE THAT NEVER WENT OUT

In the summer of 1939, the movement was picking up traction. Peter's first rally in June of that year saw a promising 350 in attendance. The next meeting, a mere two weeks later, exploded in size and a whopping 1500 crowded to hear Peter speak. Word was getting out.

All of this raised some eyebrows in the mob of course, and Anastasia and his union boss brother Tough Tony applied the thumb screws to the labour leaders. Something had to be done about Panto. Intimidation, threats, smear campaigns—all were used to put the fear of the mob into Panto, but none had any effect. Panto was just one of those people born to achieve something, it seems. He could no more stop his fight for right than a tree can stop growing.

On the evening of July 14, 1939, three members of Murder Inc.—Mendy Weiss, Tony Romanello and James Ferraco—paid a visit to Panto and hustled him from his home into a waiting car. Panto battled like a demon, biting into Mendy Weiss' finger— apparently he hit bone—but it was all for nought, of course. After all, this was Murder Incorporated. After the three thugs garrotted Panto, they dumped his body into a pit of quicklime.

When Panko did not return home, angered friends, relatives and stevedores demanded that something finally be done about things. The phrase "Where is Peter Panto?" was taken up by protestors and simple dockyard workers alike, the question scrawled on the walls of the wharfs.

In January of 1941 Panto's remains finally showed up and

everyone understood just what exactly had happened to Peter Panto. Though he hadn't stopped corruption and mob involvement in his lifetime, Peter helped light a fire that could now never go out. "Where is Peter Panto?" He's in the hearts of all those who stand against injustice and against the mob.

# IRVING "PUGGY" FEINSTEIN
## SEPTEMBER 5, 1939

### MURDER INCORPORATED GETS THE CHAIR

Irving "Puggy" Feinstein put up a heck of a fight. In fact Feinstein, an ex-boxer, bit several chunks from the finger of "Pittsburgh Phil" Harry Strauss, but it just wasn't enough. Of course, Feinstein didn't really have much of a chance. He had been lured to a meeting by three of Murder Incorporated's most notorious killers, and these were guys who took a great deal of pride in their work.

Feinstein was strictly low-level, a bottom-feeder who could have happily spent a long and fulfilling career running second-rate rackets out of Brooklyn if not for one mistake he made some time in the late 1930s. Apparently he ripped off Vincent "The Executioner" Mangano, who was top dog of the Mangano family. People don't generally walk away from things like that.

Whatever it was that Feinstein did is now lost to history, but it probably consisted of working in an unauthorized territory or not paying street tax. Anyway, the offence was grievous enough to have Mangano underboss Albert Anastasia himself put the finger on Feinstein. And that was it—Feinstein's days were now strictly limited edition.

Murder Incorporated sent its best, its most prolific boys to take care of Feinstein; and the best, of course, meant the worst. Irving's killers are known to have been Martin Goldstein, Abe

"Kid Twist" Reles and naturally Pittsburgh Phil, the most hated members of the murder-for-hire clique. Phil especially was a fiend, and used to volunteer for as many jobs as he could, just for kicks.

Poor Feinstein. He was brought to Reles's house and murdered by the ghastly trio, supposedly while Reles's mother-in-law was in an adjoining room. The elderly lady must have been very deaf, or how she could have missed all the commotion is anybody's guess.

During the proceedings Feinstein battled for his life, but taking chunks out of Pittsburgh Phil's finger was a very unfortunate move, because it just made his death all the more tortuous. At last, when Feinstein was no more, the trio of murderers took his pitiful remains out and burned them.

### THE NAME OF THAT TUNE

After that, though Feinstein was gone, he most certainly was not forgotten. In 1940, when Abe Reles sang a swan song about the doings of Goldstein, Phil and Murder Incorporated, the spectre of Irving Feinstein rose again. The gorillas of Murder Inc. were accused of Feinstein's murder as well as countless others (it's said Pittsburgh Phil alone killed at least one hundred people).

During the ensuing trials, the once handsome and dapper "Pittsburgh Phil" Strauss decided to play the insanity card and showed up to court dirty, unshaven and mumbling. Every once in a while Phil, who had never been to Pittsburgh, would try to take a bite out of his lawyer's briefcase for added effect, but it was all for nought. Goldstein and Phil were found guilty and along with other members of the murder club—Harry "Happy" Maione, Frank "The Dasher" Abbandando, Louis Capone (no relation), and Louis Buchalter—went to keep an appointment with Sing Sing's "Old Sparky"—the electric chair. Of course that didn't bring back Irving "Puggy" Feinstein, but it did bring down the final curtain on Murder Incorporated.

# EDWARD "EASY EDDIE" O'HARE
## NOVEMBER 8, 1939

### THE MAN WHO BROUGHT DOWN CAPONE

In 1932 the mighty Al Capone—Chicago's Public Enemy Number One, and perhaps the most notorious gangster of all time—was sent up for tax evasion. After the bloody calling card that was the St. Valentine's Day Massacre, the Feds were very motivated to bring Capone in, but not just any old way. No, they wanted something that would stick, a charge that would send Big Al up for good, or at least long enough to neutralize his power. So IRS Agent Frank Wilson came up with the plan of targeting Capone's income as a means of bringing him down. It was a brilliant scheme, and for Capone, ultimately inescapable.

And that's where Edward O'Hare comes into the picture. O'Hare, otherwise known as "Easy Eddie", was a mob lawyer and business manager for Capone. He was also as crooked as they come. O'Hare was not only partnered in a lot of the rackets in the South Side, but he was also privy to some very interesting details regarding Big Al's books, business transactions and the code that all this information was written in.

When he saw the zeal with which the IRS was pursuing Capone, O'Hare didn't have to give it much thought. In a heartbeat, he sold Capone down the river.

### THE DIRTY RAT

The story goes that O'Hare had a very good reason for betraying Capone, even an altruistic one. It seems that he did this terrible deed so that his son Butch would be allowed to attend Annapolis, the highly prestigious naval academy, without fear of reprisal or expulsion.

It may be true that Annapolis was part of the bargain, but undoubtedly O'Hare also received other rewards for this act of treason, such as immunity for one. After all, if Capone was going down, then it was time for all good rats to jump ship—starting with the sneakiest one.

While still working for Capone, and making money from the dog track they owned together, plus all the other Outfit rackets that O'Hare was involved in, he provided the IRS with all the information they needed to form a case against Big Al. But that's not all O'Hare did. Learning that the Outfit had got to the jury for Capone's trial, he contacted Agent Wilson with this interesting bit of news. So at the last minute Capone's jury was switched out with a new one, and Capone ended up in Alcatraz.

Miraculously, O'Hare somehow managed to survive for a number of years. But on November 8, 1939, eight days before Capone was scheduled for release, O'Hare was shot while driving his Lincoln along Ogden Avenue. The killers were never identified.

As a curious side note, O'Hare's son Butch went on to become one of the greatest war heroes of the Second World War. In fact, Chicago's O'Hare International Airport is named after him. In this case the apple fell pretty darned far from the tree.

# 4 THE FORTIES, FIFTIES AND SIXTIES: CRIME GROWS UP

**By the 1940s, '50s and '60s, the tommy-gun battles that marked earlier decades were officially over for the most part and it could now be said that organized crime was wearing a suit and tie. The Mafia and all its associate gangs of various nationalities had their fingers in quite a number of respectable enterprises and organized crime was like a business.**

But that doesn't mean that the mob had lost its teeth, not by a long shot. The way that Bugsy Siegel and Albert the "Lord High Executioner" Anastasia himself were removed from the picture showed that no one was so big they were safe. And then, of course, there was the rumoured Mafia involvement in the assassination of President Kennedy in Dallas, in November of 1963.

# ABE "KID TWIST" RELES
## NOVEMBER 12, 1941

### THE CANARY WHO COULD SING BUT COULDN'T FLY

Abe "Kid Twist" Reles was a high roller in the Syndicate's assassination wing, Murder Incorporated. Louis Buchalter, Jacob Shapiro and Albert Anastasia ran the organization, but Reles and his gang—the Boys from Brownsville—were the main executioners. When someone needed rubbing out, Reles and his boys did it with relish. But Reles also has another claim to fame: he's the stool pigeon who finally brought down the murder squad.

Reles and his gang liked to ply their trade in creative ways. Generally contracting for out-of-town killings so that they couldn't be traced to the victim, the group would tail the mark for a while before getting down to the hit. Once ready, they would use a variety of methods to get the job done—Reles favoured using an ice pick, for instance.

So good was the assassination squad that they became notorious during the 1930s and it's believed that Murder Inc. was responsible for nearly one thousand killings, many of them unsolved. All that changed in 1940, though, when Reles found himself implicated in a murder dating all the way back to 1933.

### LOOSE LIPS

Hauled up on murder charges, it didn't take long for Reles to decide what to do. Facing conviction and execution, Reles concluded his best bet was to name names, a lot of names—*all* the names. Thanks to Reles and his near-eidetic memory, the authorities were able to close a lot of gaps, lowering the boom on Mendy Weiss, Louis Capone, Dasher Abbandando, and even Louis Buchalter himself, to name but a few. All of the aforementioned got the chair.

And Reles wasn't done yet. He was about to put the finger on Albert Anastasia as well—though not if Anastasia himself had anything to say about it, of course.

Reles was being sequestered at the Half Moon Hotel on Coney Island. There was practically a brigade of cops keeping an eye on the mobster. But that didn't stop Reles from falling to his death from a window of the hotel on the morning of November 12, 1941. Coincidentally, or not, he died the day before he was to testify against Anastasia.

The official ruling of the time was that Reles had climbed out of the window—either as a prank or to try to escape—and that he'd accidentally fallen. But nobody actually believes that. It's far more plausible that Anastasia bought off the cops and had his men enter and take care of Reles or the cops had done the job themselves. The mug-shots of Reles before his death show a man whose eyes are round with terror. Reles was a marked man and he knew it.

After his literal fall from grace, Reles became known as "the canary who could sing but couldn't fly". And the charges against Albert Anastasia? With Reles no longer around to testify, they were dropped.

*Journalists prepare to photograph the body of Carlo Tresca.*

# CARLO TRESCA
## JANUARY 11, 1943

### THE MOB AND MUSSOLINI

High-profile public and political figures—the Mafia tends to avoid killing these. Ever since the anti-Italian backlash that accompanied the death of Captain David Hennessy in 1890 (possibly a Mafia murder), La Cosa Nostra has steered clear of the politicos. The consequences are just too high.

There are a couple of notable exceptions to this rule, however, just like everything to do with the Mafia. One of these exceptions probably occurred in Dallas in 1963. Enough has been written on that assassination to fill a whole bookstore and there is compelling evidence to suggest Mafia involvement in the murder of JFK. Another death, one that took place in 1943, was undeniably a Mafia slaying—the murder of Carlo Tresca.

Tresca was an Italian-born anarchist, newspaper editor and activist. Born in Sulmona, Tresca had fled Italy in 1904 to avoid impending arrest, bringing his ideals and strength of purpose with him.

Tresca was a principled man, one who fought ceaselessly for his beliefs—empowerment of workers, justice for the down-trodden and, of course, the ideologies of anarchism. Tall and handsome, he was a riveting speaker, and a powerful voice against Fascism for Italian-Americans. This was particularly important throughout the 1930s and the opening years of the Second World War.

Tresca's fiery oratories undoubtedly made certain factions uncomfortable, though, both in the United States and in Italy. Mussolini reportedly sent Fascist operatives to deal with Tresca in 1926, using bombs. They failed.

### MAKING ENEMIES

But Tresca had his fair share of enemies in the United States as well, among them Frank Garofalo, underboss of the Bonanno family. Tresca wrote fervently against the Mafia, and shortly before he died had penned a piece that brought Garofalo to task. Tresca knew he was at risk; he had lived with danger all his life. Ultimately, though, he could only be what he was—tireless and crusading.

Inevitably his outspokenness brought Tresca to his death. On January 11, 1943, he left his newspaper office at around 9:45 in the evening. Just as he crossed the road, a black car pulled up beside him and a man in a trenchcoat got out. Moments later, Carlo Tresca was lying dead in the street, a bullet in his head. And that was that.

For a long time the murder of Tresca was considered a mystery, with speculation veering between Fascist agents operating in America or Italian communists. But the assassination was very well orchestrated, smooth and clean. Historians now know that the murder of Carlo Tresca was a Mafia hit. In fact, the evidence is fairly clear as to who the man in the trenchcoat was that dark January evening—Carmine "Lilo" Galante, decades before his audacious takeover of the Bonanno family. In the death of Tresca, Galante would have been operating under orders from Frank Garofalo, and therefore Joseph Bonanno himself.

But Tresco's achievements demand that he be remembered for far more than the way he died. He was a man of worth, one who stood his ground, and not just another notch on the gun of Carmine Galante.

# WILLIAM "DINTY" COLBECK
## FEBRUARY 17, 1943

### EGAN'S RATS

William "Dinty" Colbeck was a member of St. Louis's notorious Egan's Rats during the Roaring Twenties. Fiercely loyal to boss William Egan, Colbeck had done a stint in the Great War. After serving with the 89th Infantry Division, he took the skills he'd learned in battle and put them to use for the gang. Unfortunately it was Colbeck and his itchy trigger finger that engulfed St. Louis in a gang war that left the city reeling.

St. Louis in the early 1920s was divided between several gangs—Egan's Rats, the Cuckoos, and the Hogan Gang being the main mobs. The Rats were the dominant gang and lorded it over the others in their bootlegging and bank robbery enterprises. In 1921, though, a couple of Hogan men decided to put an end to all that and took out Rat leader William Egan. Colbeck was shortly on the scene and, reputedly hearing Egan's last words, could name his killers. Now, this may have been true, or it may have been a convenient way for Colbeck to assume the mantle of leadership. In any case Colbeck was determined—Egan's death meant war.

St. Louis was a war zone, and members of both mobs shot it out on the streets, running down anyone unlucky enough to get in their way. Costs were mounting too, and Colbeck soon found that the Rats' bootlegging funds were drying up. The gang took to bank robbing and postal holdups to rustle up some funds, but it was clear that Colbeck was not the boss that Egan had been, not by a long shot. Unable to command anywhere near the loyalty that the old boss had, Colbeck found himself increasingly isolated and paranoia set in. As a pastime, Colbeck took to picking off his own men.

### RATTING ON THE RATS
When Rat member Ray Renard was arrested for robbery, then, he figured he had nothing to lose and likely everything to gain by spilling the beans—and there were a lot of beans. Based on Renard's statements, Colbeck and the core of the gang were sentenced to twenty-five years.

Colbeck lingered in prison until 1940, when at last he was paroled and out on the streets again. With the sweet smell of freedom in his lungs once more, Colbeck got to thinking that maybe he could pick up where he'd left off; rule St. Louis once more, put the old gang back together.

But like so many others before him, Colbeck didn't realize that too much had vanished since 1924. The mobs didn't operate the same way, that was for sure, and none of the current hoods felt like making room for Dinty Colbeck.

Really, Colbeck should have known what was coming next. On the night of February 17, 1943, he was gunned down while driving his car on Destrehan Street. With the demise of Colbeck and with the other Rats either dead, in prison or moved on, St. Louis had seen the last of Egan's Rats.

# ROCCO PERRI
## APRIL 23, 1944

### CANADA'S GREATEST BOOTLEGGER

Self-styled as "Canada's greatest bootlegger", Rocco Perri was brazen about the title. He would hold court in his home in Hamilton, Ontario, granting interviews to newspapers and flaunting his position to the cops. And what's more, he was able to get away with it.

The thing was that though Perri admitted to being a bootlegger, that admission alone was not enough, under Canadian law, to put him behind bars. The cops required some proof; Perri had to be caught in the act in order to make the charges stick. During the 1920s that just hadn't happened. Though Rocco did a little time in 1927 for perjury, there wasn't much more than that to bring him in.

It's hardly remembered today, but a form of Prohibition existed throughout the late teens and into the 1920s in a number of Canadian provinces. The problem, at least as far as the temperance organizations were concerned, was that the ban was not nationwide. Certain provinces, such as Quebec, voted Prohibition down pretty sharply, while the provinces that did maintain it had a confusing array of laws in place that allowed for loopholes and, frankly, defiance. Perri took advantage of these slim regulations and shipped the good stuff not only into the United States, but sold it in Canada as well, making double the money.

## CHANGING TIMES

Perri's partner in crime in all this was his common-law wife, Bessie Starkman, a formidable woman who was one of the few females to hold sway during the heyday of organized crime. Some claim that she was the actual force behind the throne of the Perri empire, that Perri rarely acted without her instructions.

This seems unlikely, however, as Bessie was thoroughly disliked by the Perri goons, and lacked the finesse, charisma and people skills to run the Perri organization. Bessie was so disliked in fact that on August 13, 1930, she was killed, probably by members of the Perri establishment. Perri, heartbroken and almost collapsing at the cemetery, gave Bessie a lavish send-off worthy of any mob boss of the period. And then he went right back to work.

Throughout the 1930s Perri aligned himself with another strong woman, Annie Newman, and branched out into extortion, gambling and other rackets. But it would be the Second World War that finally took the wind out of his sails. Frank Zaneth, an operative in the RCMP who had been hounding Perri for years, was at last able to apprehend the gangster under the War Measures Act, arresting him as a suspected Fascist and enemy alien. It was an excuse, of course, a loophole that allowed Zaneth to bring the mobster in. Perri was well acquainted with loopholes.

He didn't get out again until 1943, and like so many other mobsters before him, found that things had changed since he'd been in jail—Petawawa this time. For one thing, the Buffalo family—the Magaddinos—had expanded their territory into Perri's old stomping ground of Hamilton, Ontario.

So on the balmy spring morning of April 23, 1944, Perri went out for a walk, and was never seen again. Some said he had just "disappeared" himself, and actually survived into the early 1950s.

It's more likely, however, that Perri was given cement overshoes and is currently residing at the bottom of Hamilton Bay. The Magaddinos then had nothing to worry about.

# LAWRENCE MANGANO
## AUGUST 3, 1944

### MANGANO AND THE BIG TUNA

"Dago" Lawrence Mangano was a member of the Chicago Outfit. In charge of the Near West Side, he quietly rose through the ranks until he found himself almost on a par with the ambitious Anthony "Big Tuna" Accardo. That, of course, was a situation that couldn't last long.

Mangano dealt with gambling in the 1930s, a goldmine for gangs once Prohibition had been repealed. At the end of his life he would be branded Public Enemy Number Four, at a time when the United States, and Chicago especially, was awash with gangsters. In fact, Mangano was only a few notches below Outfit boss Frank Nitti, and he was no pushover.

Like so many mobsters of the time, Mangano had the cops in his pocket—all except one, Captain Luke Garrick. Mangano took care of Garrick, though—one day in 1928, the captain's home was destroyed by a bomb. After that Garrick, who survived the blast, fell nicely in line like all the others. It was a minor incident in the career of Mangano, but it shows what he was capable of.

### THE HOLLYWOOD SCANDAL

But in 1941 the Chicago Outfit began to implode. They'd been shaking down the Hollywood moguls, demanding money to ensure the entertainment unions wouldn't strike. The revelation of this racket caused quite a stir, especially when top Hollywood figures such as Harry Warner of Warner Brothers testified.

Frank Nitti began to lose his grip at the thought of having to go back to prison again. He suffered from claustrophobia, and he just couldn't bear the idea of being caged in a confined space. So on March 19, 1943, Nitti blew his brains out.

Paul Ricca and Louis Campagna, also top men in the Outfit, were brought down by the Hollywood scandal, and were packed off to prison. The setback to the Outfit was staggering. That really only left Tony Accardo and Lawrence Mangano as the top contenders for Al Capone's old crown.

The end for Mangano came on the summery evening of August 3, 1944. He had been out on the town with Mike Pontelli, his chauffeur (and that also meant bodyguard) and Pontelli's then girlfriend, Rita Reyes. As the group was heading home, driving along in Mangano's car, Mangano noticed a vehicle following behind them.

Not worried in the least, Mangano thought it was just the cops looking for a shakedown; he could easily buy them off. So on Mangano's instructions, Pontelli pulled the car over and stopped. Mangano got out, money in hand, but when the other car pulled up, the occupants opened fire and splattered Mangano all over the road. Circling around, they came back and finished off Pontelli too.

Mangano survived, but not for long. Astoundingly, there were around two hundred shotgun pellets in his body, plus several slugs. That night Lawrence Mangano closed his eyes for the last time. And with the death of Mangano, Tony Accardo was uncontested in his bid for leadership of the Chicago Outfit.

# JAMES RAGEN
## AUGUST 15, 1946

### HIGH-PLACED CRIME

James Ragen was an anachronism from the rough-and-tumble days of the Teens and Twenties who held his own against larger and more sophisticated groups in Chicago. A co-founder of the athletic club/street mob Ragen's Colts, he steadfastly remained an independent when that gang was absorbed into the Syndicate via the Chicago Outfit in the 1930s.

After Prohibition was repealed in 1933 the mobs concentrated their efforts largely on gambling to supply the vast funds that booze had once given them. One such source of revenue was provided by the General News Service, which swiftly communicated gambling and racing results to the entire country. With instantaneous race results wired throughout the nation, bookies had inside knowledge of racing winners while they were still taking bets. The possibilities for profit were enormous. Run in the 1930s by publisher Moses Annenberg with Ragen as his assistant, the service was worth a fortune.

In 1939, though, Annenberg was indicted for tax evasion and sold the racing wire to Ragen. Though the mob may have had a foothold in the service during Annenberg's day, Ragen was determined to run the operation without Syndicate interference and rake in the profits for himself. He became one of the most powerful gambling figures in the country.

The smell of filthy lucre inevitably brought the Syndicate. During a time when supposedly a twelve-year-old couldn't slice bread in Chicago without the mob's say-so, there was no way the Outfit was going to let an independent like Ragen get the better of them.

### NO HELP FROM THE FEDS

At first the mob attempted to start rival wire services, then to buy Ragen out. But when neither of these plans panned out, the Outfit got serious. Ragen was wily, he'd survived for years on the mean streets of Chicago and he knew how the mob operated. So he contacted journalist Drew Pearson; Ragen had a story to tell.

Pearson communicated with the FBI and when the Feds took down Regan's statements they found out just how deeply entrenched the Outfit was in all of Chicago's day-to-day businesses. The mob had representatives everywhere, some of them very highly placed. The information was dynamite, but it apparently went nowhere.

It seemed as if the Feds were sitting on their hands. Backing away from Ragen, they claimed that the responsibility for the Chicago Outfit rested with the city of Chicago itself—in other words it was a municipal and not a federal problem.

Ragen's next move was to hire bodyguards, but it wasn't enough and on June 24, 1946 he was shot while driving down the street in his car. Much to the dismay of the Outfit no doubt, Ragen survived this first assault and was taken to hospital, but while trying to recuperate he died suddenly on August 15. The coroner stated that a vial's worth of mercury had been found in Ragen's stomach, an amount sufficient to kill three men. But no murder charges could be brought, apparently, because of the slim and incomprehensible reason that it could not be ascertained whether Ragen had died as a result of the gunshots, or the mercury poisoning. Crime in high places indeed.

Benjamin "Bugsy" Siegel's dead body lying on a divan in his Beverly Hills home in 1947.

# BENJAMIN "BUGSY" SIEGEL
## JUNE 20, 1947

### ALWAYS FRONT PAGE NEWS

There's a picture of Bugsy Siegel, one of those famous mug shots that sums up the racketeer so succinctly—Siegel, smirking at the dumb flatfoots taking his picture, his eyes hooded. It could be a picture of an actor in a movie role, someone playing a gangster. Looking at Siegel, you know you're looking at the big time, 1940s style. He exuded charisma and he also exuded "mobster".

Handsome enough to be a Hollywood A-lister, Siegel was also a prominent member of the Syndicate and one of the most feared gangsters of his time. And heaven help anyone who actually called him "Bugsy" to his face—he hated the name.

Knee-deep in the Hollywood lifestyle—parties, nightclubs and starlets—Siegel was called "Bugsy" because he was more than a bit nuts. But make no mistake—he wasn't afraid to put himself on the front line. Referred to by one old-time mobster as one of the gutsiest guys he'd ever met, Siegel had reputedly been one of the hired guns who'd eliminated boss of all bosses Salvatore Maranzano—the *capo di tutti capi* himself.

### HIGH STAKES

But one of Siegel's greatest achievements was the creation of Las Vegas, Nevada as a gambling mecca. It wasn't really his idea, though—it was actually newspaper owner William Wilkerson who first realized a fortune could be made out there in the desert where men were men and gambling was legal. All that was needed was a nice casino or two, destination spots that would bring out high rollers and casual gamblers alike. In 1945 Wilkerson began construction on the Flamingo Hotel, a resort that was to echo the high-class casinos of Europe.

But by 1946 Wilkerson had run out of funds and the Flamingo still wasn't finished. Siegel swooped in and bought Wilkerson out, continuing construction on something that was to be even more sumptuous than the newspaperman had first imagined. Borrowing heavily from his pals (and that means the mob), Siegel was now spending over six million dollars on the Flamingo—an astronomical figure in those days.

The grand opening in December of 1946 was less than Siegel had hoped for, though. With a small turnout and construction work still going on, the festivities were something of a bust and the casino was losing money. Of course it didn't help that Siegel was skimming money off the club's profits, but then that was a mob habit.

Siegel took a step back and regrouped. Staving off polite requests from his associates for a return on their investments, Siegel started a public relations campaign that would get the word out on the Flamingo and turn things around sharply. When the club reopened two months later, it looked as if his plan was going to pay off.

The Flamingo was now in the black and gaining in popularity. It was too bad that Siegel wouldn't be around to enjoy it. On the evening of June 20, 1947, while sitting in the living room of his girlfriend's mansion, Bugsy Siegel was shot dead by an unknown gunman who blasted through the windows. Though Siegel's killer has never been identified, it's probable his murder was ordered by the Syndicate's pre-eminent gambling controller, Meyer Lansky. There was that little matter of the skimming, and the debt just tied the whole thing up with a bow. The Flamingo cost a heck of a lot, far more than Siegel had bargained for.

# CHARLES BINAGGIO
## APRIL 5, 1950

### KANSAS CITY CONNECTION

Charles Binaggio was a mobster and political fixer in Kansas City. Originally attached to the corrupt but effective James Pendergast political machine, Binaggio broke out on his own in the mid-1940s when the Pendergast ship began to sink.

Backing his own man for governor—Forrest Smith—Binaggio had plans for Missouri, lots of plans. First, he wanted to get control of the police forces of Kansas City and St. Louis—just a few men in highly placed positions. Once he had the cops in his pocket, Binaggio intended to open the state wide open to gambling.

Putting the word around, Binaggio took up subscriptions—mob money—to get his man into position and in 1948 Forrest Smith became Governor of Missouri. Now everything was in place—pretty soon there'd be plenty of loot to go around.

### THE DOUBLECROSS

There would have been, except it now seemed that suddenly Forrest Smith was developing a conscience. It couldn't have come at a worse time.

Some sources indicate that Smith began to stall Binaggio regarding the gambling, telling him that he would have to wait six months for the new administration to get its sea legs. Other sources say that Smith went even further, and actually blocked Binaggio's Police Board choices. Whatever the tactic, the gambling plans had to be put on the shelf. There were now a lot of very unhappy gamblers demanding that somebody pay. Binaggio was about to find out what the price would be.

Binaggio spent the afternoon of April 5, 1950 in his garden, pottering around his roses. After dinner he said farewell to his wife and daughter and headed to the Last Chance Tavern, an establishment he partly owned. According to Binaggio's body-guard, Nick Penna, at around 8 p.m. Binaggio received a call and then excused himself. Taking his second-in-command, Charles "Mad Dog" Gargotta, with him, Binaggio told Penna that he'd only be gone for about twenty minutes. Penna was never to see Binaggio alive again.

The next morning the bodies of Binaggio and Gargotta were found sprawled in one of the rooms of the Democratic Club on Truman Road. Running water had alerted a cabbie to the scene, and the police were called in.

So who shot Binaggio? The theory is that the killing was likely an outside job—some contract killer brought in from New York or Chicago. The hit certainly looked professional—four clean shots fired point blank at Binaggio's head. Gargotta had put up more of a fight apparently and had made a run for the door. But it was futile. A single shot had stopped Gargotta in his tracks and then the murderer had moved in for the kill. That saw the end of the political career of Charles Binaggio.

# VINCENT MANGANO
## APRIL 19, 1951

### THE EXECUTIONER

Vincent "The Executioner" Mangano was boss of one of New York's five Mafia families. But there was also another "Executioner" in the Mangano family—Albert Anastasia. These two together in the same gang never saw eye to eye, and since Anastasia was also one of the leaders of Murder Incorporated, it was a foregone conclusion which executioner would come out on top.

The Mangano mob made its wealth through gambling, labour racketeering and the waterfront. In fact Mangano controlled the waterfront, through Anastasia and his labour boss brother "Tough Tony" Anastasia. Because of the two brothers, all goods coming into port on a daily basis were pretty much up for grabs and Mangano could lift whatever he wanted.

So, here's the rub—Mangano severely resented Anastasia's moonlighting for the murder squad. He undoubtedly also felt threatened by Anastasia's elevated position in the group, one which allowed him to pal around with Lucky Luciano and Frank Costello, to name just two. Stories are told as to how Mangano and Anastasia would verbally duke it out on a regular basis, sometimes nearly coming to blows. But both knew the score—best to lie low for the time being and put up with things as long as it was convenient. It was just a matter of time, though, as to who would strike first. This prickly state of affairs lasted until 1951.

## THE TAKEOVER

Later, Anastasia claimed that Mangano had forced him to do it, that Mangano had put out a contract on him and had left him no choice. Other than that, Anastasia had nothing to say, not to the police, nor the Commission. But everybody knew the real score. In the battle for the Manganos, Anastasia had staged a little family coup.

The first to go was Mangano's brother Philip, naturally enough also in the mob. His waterlogged body was found in a marsh in Jamaica Bay on April 19, 1951. He had been shot three times. Later that same day it was pretty clear that Vincent was also missing. Both Mangano brothers were gone within hours of each other. The body of Vincent "The Executioner" has never surfaced.

Now Anastasia had to move swiftly to consolidate his position. Meeting with the Commission, Anastasia, backed by Frank Costello, persuaded the group to give him control of the Mangano family. He must have been pretty convincing because when he left the table that day, the entity known as the Mangano family was history—it had just become the Anastasia family. Albert "The Executioner" Anastasia had arrived.

# ANTHONY BRANCATO & ANTHONY TROMBINO
## AUGUST 6, 1951

### THE TWO TONYS

Loose and wild, the Two Tonys were desperados, living auda-ciously—and they died sprawled out in the front seat of a car somewhere near Hollywood Boulevard in one of the most infamous hits in mob history.

Tony Brancato was largely regarded as just a low-level hood from Kansas City, but that's not how he saw it. As far as he was concerned, he was going places and Kansas City just wasn't big enough to hold him. That's why he headed over to the bright lights and fast times in Los Angeles to work for Mickey Cohen, one of the big cheeses out there in LA. His brother Norfia also worked for Cohen and there seemed a prospect that Norfia could get him a real sweet gig out there.

As soon as Tony Brancato hit the coast, he began to make himself unpopular, muscling in on other people's rackets and generally stirring up a lot of noise. It wouldn't do. Cohen had a lot of prob-lems of his own, what with tax charges and a war with another LA mobster, Jack Dragna. For Cohen, control of the entire city was at stake, and he didn't have time to babysit Norfia's little brother.

So Tony Brancato struck out on his own for a bit, did a little freelancing, not really getting anywhere. Then he got the brilliant idea of bringing his old pal Tony Trombino down from Kansas City. Once Trombino hit the town, things started to come together and the two pals let loose, getting into everything: robbery, narcotics, murder. They were even suspected of the murder of Bugsy Siegel—but so were a lot of others. Leaving a trail behind them a mile wide, the Tonys didn't care how they pulled off their jobs and it showed. By the end of their career they had been arrested a total of forty-six times.

The two Tonys never seemed to realize that there were some targets that should be considered off limits. One case in point: on May 28, 1951 the Tonys, and some other gangsters, held up the sports betting concern of the Flamingo Hotel. The total haul of the heist was $3,500. It was not much of a paycheque, but the truth was that with the Flamingo job, the Tonys had now officially bitten off more than they could chew.

The Flamingo had been built by Bugsy Siegel, and although by now he was well and truly dead, the joint was unquestionably a mobbed-up operation. Basically then, the Tonys had just ripped off the mob. After that Jack Dragna got into the picture and it was pretty much a done deal as far as the Tonys were concerned.

Jimmy "The Weasel" Fratianno was given the contract, along with Charlie "Bats" Battaglia. And on the night of August 6, 1951, the end came for the two Tonys as they sat in their car, waiting to hear the details of a big score that was supposedly coming their way. It was just a lure of course, something to dangle in front of the Tonys so they could get whacked.

The cops never found out who killed Brancato and Trombino until Fratianno flipped in 1977 and named the Tonys as just one of the hits he'd done. It's to be hoped the Tonys enjoyed that $3,500.

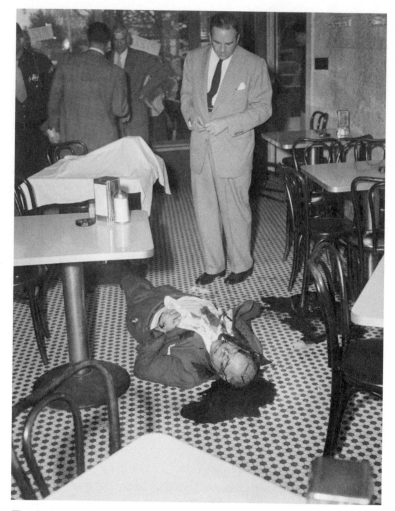

The body of Willie Moretti at "Joe's Restaurant," Oct. 4th, 1951. Looking down at the body is Bergen County Attorney General Nelson Stamler, a long-time friend of rackets kingpin Joe Adonis, and his brother, Salvatore, who is Adonis' lieutenant.

# GUARINO "WILLIE" MORETTI
## OCTOBER 4, 1951

### THE RAT PACK PALS

Guarino "Willie" Moretti was quite a card. If there was any humour at all in a situation he could find it. He loved a good story and was known to tell quite a few in his time. So when the Kefauver Hearings started in 1950 and suspected Mafia members were called in to testify, Moretti found that he just couldn't help himself—some stories were just too good to keep under his hat. And that's when Vito Genovese took it upon himself to cut Moretti off in mid-sentence.

Moretti had long been a member of the Luciano family and was quite a respected "made man". It's said he was pals with such luminaries as Dean Martin, Jerry Lewis and Frank Sinatra. In fact the story goes that when Sinatra was trying to break his contract with Tommy Dorsey but the band leader wouldn't agree, Moretti showed up at Dorsey's and stuck a gun down his throat to change his mind. Needless to say, Sinatra was released from his contract. No doubt Moretti had a great laugh over that one.

Unfortunately, Moretti liked to have a good time a little too much. Some time during his life, what with all the parties and in general living it up, Moretti had contracted syphilis. For years, though, he was able to keep his illness under control and act as an effective mafioso.

### THE MERCY KILLING

But by the time the Kefauver Hearings began, Moretti had definitely gone into decline. Syphilis causes mental degeneration and admittedly Moretti's behaviour was becoming aberrant. He'd started to bet on imaginary horse races and to ramble on endlessly when telling his famous stories. When other mobsters such as Frank Costello and Meyer Lansky were called to testify at the Hearings, each one refused, pleading the Fifth Amendment. Moretti, however, seemed to treat the Kefauver Hearings as a bit of a lark, a chance to show off and have some fun. He had the senators at the hearings in stitches on more than one occasion. Clearly Moretti was starting to falter. Who could say what secrets he might give away?

It was Vito Genovese who went to the Commission for permission to put Moretti down. The argument was bitter, but in the end it was decided—Moretti had to be dealt with and his death would be a mercy killing. But of course Genovese had another motive: with Moretti out of the way, he would be one step closer to total control of the Luciano family.

On October 4, 1951 Willie Moretti met some friends for brunch at Joe's Elbow Room. He had quite a pleasant day planned and was even expecting to meet up with Dean Martin and Jerry Lewis later. However, some time during the course of the meal, when the wait staff were conveniently in the kitchen, Moretti's companions pulled out their guns and put an end to him. It's said that he was hit a number of times in the face and that such shots were signs of respect. With friends like that, who needs enemies?

# ALBERT "THE MAD HATTER" ANASTASIA
## OCTOBER 25, 1957

### THEY DO IT WITH MIRRORS

Albert Anastasia was known as "The Mad Hatter" and "The Lord High Executioner". A past big shot of Murder Incorporated, by 1951 he had risen to the position of Godfather and was now one of the most powerful bosses in America. Of course he'd had to kill off his old boss Vincent Mangano to get there, but who was counting?

His elevated status had been a long time coming and a lot of bodies had floated under the bridge—Vincent and Philip Mangano to name but two—but finally the truly merciless Anastasia could say he was at the top of the heap. His position as boss, however, was far from secure. Things were heating up among the Families and there was one man within Anastasia's own mob who may have been even more dangerous than The Executioner himself, if that was possible—Carlo Gambino.

Among Anastasia's rivals outside of his gang was Vito Genovese, who had his own designs on the old Luciano mob, now run by Frank Costello. Genovese needed Costello dead. The only problem was, Costello and Anastasia were pretty thick and Genovese couldn't make a move on Costello without fear of Anastasia lowering the boom.

That's when Genovese started to get chummy with Anastasia's underling, Gambino. Anastasia was erratic and overly violent, Genovese said. What's more he'd likely sold off Mafia positions and couldn't be trusted. Gambino undoubtedly didn't need much convincing when it came to dealing with Anastasia. After all, with him gone there would be nothing to stop Gambino from taking over the entire Anastasia family. It's all like something from the court of a Neapolitan prince—murder, betrayal and intrigue.

Things began to move fast in 1957. In May of that year an assassination attempt was made on Frank Costello. As a consequence Costello suddenly found he had a new outlook on life and stepped down as head of the Luciano family. Now all that remained as far as Gambino was concerned was to take care of Anastasia himself.

### A SHAVE AND A HAIRCUT

It happened on October 25, 1957. Anastasia was sitting in the barber shop of the Park Sheraton Hotel waiting for a shave and a haircut. As he relaxed in the chair, steaming towels over his face, two men muscled their way into the shop, their guns drawn. Seeing that he was in danger, Anastasia lunged forward in an attempt to attack his assailants, but what he thought was the gunmen turned out to be their reflections in the mirror. He had merely dived at an illusion. The gunmen, meanwhile, opened fire and the helpless Anastasia fell dead on the linoleum tiles of the barber shop floor.

After dealing out death so liberally and for so many years, Albert "The Mad Hatter" Anastasia, the "Lord High Executioner" himself finally got his. Not long after, the old Anastasia mob was rechristened the Gambino family. Anastasia had met with a fitting end.

# GUS GREENBAUM
## DECEMBER 3, 1958

### THE VEGAS CURSE
The scene was a 1950s bedroom. The shade of a chrome floor lamp hovered like a spaceship over the bed. Light from a television flickered, while the piercing "off-the-air" signal whined unendingly. Next to Greenbaum was a heating pad, something to take the chill off the night. The only thing was, Greenbaum couldn't feel that chill at the time. In fact, Greenbaum would never feel anything again, for he was dead.

It must have been the Vegas curse. That's the thing that got both Greenbaum and Bugsy Siegel. Undoubtedly many a gambler has fallen victim to the curse on some level or other—gambling away their paycheques, their mortgages, their sanity. Greenbaum and Bugsy lost more than that, though. They lost their lives.

Mere hours after Siegel was executed for mismanaging Vegas's Flamingo Hotel, the Chicago Outfit brought in Greenbaum, as well as Moe Sedway, to turn the prospect around. The pair did just that, and in spectacular fashion, bringing the casino into the black to the tune of four million dollars within the first year. Of course it helped that Siegel wasn't around to skim the profits any more.

Greenbaum seemed to have the magic touch when it came to Vegas, and the Outfit as well as Meyer Lansky liked what they saw. In 1955, Outfit boss Tony Accardo and mob accountant Jake Guzik asked Greenbaum to take over management of the Riviera as well, another mobbed-up casino that was losing money. Greenbaum, however, turned them down. He was tired of the game, he said, and wanted to rest. He was looking forward to spending the rest of his life just pottering around and living off his ill-gotten gains. "Sure," Guzik said, patting Greenbaum on the back; then the mobsters headed back to Chicago. Seven days later Greenbaum's sister-in-law was found murdered in her home. Greenbaum got the message and took over the Riviera for his good buddies in the mob.

### A HAPPY RETIREMENT

Maybe Guzik should have listened to Greenbaum though and let him retire. The strain of running things in Vegas was beginning to tell on Gus and he took to seeking out recreation—heavy recreation—that consisted of gambling (naturally enough), alcohol, narcotics and female companionship. The mob took notice of this, and though they weren't pleased, they could have overlooked all of it as long as the casinos stayed in the black. The trouble was, in order to pay for all of these expensive pastimes, Greenbaum had begun to skim from the till just like Bugsy had.

According to Johnny Roselli, it was Meyer Lansky who put the contract out on Gus Greenbaum. No surprise there—Lansky was the gambling tsar. On December 3, 1958, Greenbaum and his wife Bess were found murdered in their home, Greenbaum still curled up in front of the TV, a heating pad next to his body. It was strange that Mrs. Greenbaum had also been killed—the mob doesn't usually kill family members. Maybe Lansky just wanted to underline the message in this one—in red ink. Or maybe it was the Vegas curse.

# ABNER ZWILLMAN
## FEBRUARY 26, 1959

### THE MOB AND JEAN HARLOW

Abner Zwillman seems to be somewhat forgotten today. In his time, though, he was one of the most important mobsters in New York's underworld and a member of the Syndicate. In fact Zwillman was referred to as the Al Capone of New Jersey.

Zwillman worked the rackets, going in for gambling, labour slugging and bootlegging, with some legitimate businesses such as night clubs thrown in for kicks. Reports say that he controlled about 40 percent of all the booze that was smuggled into the United States from Canada. Now that's a lot of whisky. The Zwillman mob was making a bundle.

Zwillman also dabbled in the movie-making industry, partially running the Projectionist Union and also payrolling the overbearing movie mogul Harry Cohn. It's fairly common knowledge that Cohn had mob connections, and Zwillman lent the mogul quite a hefty sum. But the money wasn't without strings, of course. Expecting the loan to be repaid—and with plenty of interest— Zwillman also demanded that Cohn give his girlfriend a movie contract. Zwillman's girlfriend at the time was no ordinary starlet, but the original platinum blonde herself—Jean Harlow. Zwillman reputedly gave the beautiful Harlow a jewelled bracelet and a red Cadillac, among other gifts. Now that's travelling in style.

## DEAD IN THE BASEMENT

But when the 1950s came along, Zwillman, like so many other gangsters, began to feel the pinch. In mid-1950 he was called to testify at the Kefauver Hearings and from 1953 to 1956 he endured investigation, indictment and trial for tax evasion. The Feds were finally trying to get tough with organized crime, and Zwillman was one of their targets.

The heat was really on in 1959 when Zwillman was once more called to testify before a committee, this one the McClellan Senate Committee. Zwillman was reportedly despondent and there were those—Meyer Lansky for one—who feared that he would crack under the pressure and give the whole game away. Apparently Lansky went to the Syndicate.

On February 26, 1959, Zwillman was found in his basement hanging by a cord from the ceiling. The official ruling on his death was suicide—after all, Zwillman had been pretty low, what with the McClellan investigation and his recent tax troubles. But a ruling of suicide would definitely not explain the bruises that were found on his body, particularly his wrists. On the contrary, such marks seemed to indicate that the mobster had been bound prior to being killed and then strung up after death.

One story says that Lucky Luciano, now exiled and living in Italy, confirmed that Zwillman had been murdered. Maybe only Meyer Lansky could corroborate that statement, but murdered or not, Zwillman wouldn't be testifying any time soon.

# ANTHONY CARFANO
## SEPTEMBER 25, 1959

### LITTLE AUGIE PISANO

Anthony "Little Augie Pisano" Carfano went a way back. A member of the Luciano mob in the 1930s (and going back even further than that), Carfano later became a heavy hitter for Frank Costello when that mobster took over Lucky's operations. But say what you want about Augie—and a lot could be said about the man—he was one loyal son of a gun. Even when Vito Genovese was muscling Costello out of the Mafia completely, Carfano threw his lot in with his old boss—best buds to the end. The end for Carfano was about to come pretty soon if Genovese had anything to say about it.

On the evening of September 25, 1959, Carfano went to the Copacabana nightclub to unwind a little. Things had been pretty tense for him lately, what with a murder attempt on Costello and Genovese breathing down his neck. Besides, the Copacabana in New York was one of the hottest night spots in the country.

Carfano didn't go to the Copa alone, though. A former beauty queen—Janice Drake—also went with him. Actually, that name was *Mrs.* Janice Drake. Carfano and the Drakes had a long history—in fact Carfano had helped build up the career of Janice's husband, Allan. He was a second-rate comedian, but with the backing of Carfano he was getting some pretty sweet gigs. That was until Carfano ran afoul of Genovese. Then things started to dry up for Drake.

In any case, while Allan was out on the road with his act, hitting the hot spots, Carfano would check up on Janice—make sure she was coping. He would also take her out on the town. And buy her pearl bracelets. Yes, Carfano and Janice were more than just friends; you could say that the two of them were pretty tight.

## A WARNING FROM FRANK

That night—Carfano's last night—when he and Janice were enjoying the food and each other's company, he got a phone call. It's speculated that this call was from Frank Costello and he was giving his friend a heads up: "Augie, they're gunning for ya; get out of there in a hurry!" So Carfano left the Copa post-haste and he took Janice with him. The pair slipped into Carfano's car—a beautiful black Cadillac—and Carfano hit the gas. But Genovese had foreseen such a possibility, and had some torpedoes planted in the back seat of the car, waiting. Exit Little Augie Pisano.

The bodies of Carfano and Janice were found slumped in the front seats of Carfano's vehicle, which was parked somewhere near LaGuardia Airport. Carfano had fallen sideways, and Janice was next to him, her head leaning against the passenger window, her open eyes staring off at nothing. For poor Janice it had been just a case of being in the wrong place at the wrong time. As for Carfano, he had discovered the heavy price of loyalty.

# JACK WHALEN
## DECEMBER 2, 1959

### THE ENFORCER

Jack Whalen, aka Jack O'Hara, should have had everything. He stood 6ft tall and had Fifties-style matinée idol looks. Whalen could have been a movie star. He should have been a movie star. It would have been better than tangling with Mickey Cohen—one of Los Angeles' most notorious mob bosses.

Everything seemed set to work for Whalen. As a youngster, he'd gone to a private military school where he'd hobnobbed with the offspring of the wealthy and played polo in between classes. In World War II he had been a hero, a bomber pilot who'd downed his share of Nazis. And when he returned from overseas he had married into one of the richest families in Los Angeles. There was absolutely no reason why Whalen couldn't have had it all. He must just have been drawn to the seamier side of life.

Whalen was pretty tough; he could smash heads together—and often did—with the best of them. He relied on his muscle to get the job done and was so tough that he'd take care of business without using a gun. They called him "The Enforcer". Truth be told, Whalen was practically a mob all by himself.

Like others of the time, Jack Whalen had tried to muscle in on some of Mickey Cohen's territory when that gangster went to prison. This of course didn't sit too well with Mickey and by 1959 Jack had taken things too far.

## SHOOT-OUT AT RONDELLI'S

Just before midnight on December 2, 1959, Jack Whalen burst his way into Rondelli's restaurant, itching for a fight. Present at the restaurant that night were Joe Mars, George Piscitelle and Sam LoCigno, flunkies for Mickey Cohen—and Cohen himself. Whalen was looking for Piscitelle and LoCigno, he said; they owed a bookie client of his nine hundred bucks and he was there to collect.

Arriving at Cohen's table, Whalen began to rough up Piscitelle and LoCigno, demanding the dough. Shortly after that someone at the table pulled out a gun and shot Whalen right between the eyes. Whalen went down about as hard as you'd expect, and expired soon after.

So, who pulled the trigger that night? Mickey Cohen hadn't seen what had happened, or so he said. As soon as Whalen started on Piscitelle and LoCigno, Cohen had dived under the table and stayed there until things died down—literally.

During the investigation several guns were found in a trash can outside the restaurant, almost as if they'd been planted there. But what's even more interesting is that a few days after the murder, Cohen stooge LoCigno showed up at the police station and confessed to the killing. The case went to trial but try as they might, the prosecution could not pin Whalen's death on Cohen.

After a guilty verdict and an appeal LoCigno eventually got life; more than likely he also got a hefty pay-off from Cohen too. But that's a heck of a lot better than what Jack Whalen got.

# ROGER TOUHY
## DECEMBER 16, 1959

### THE FRAME-UP

Roger Touhy's story sounds like a Hollywood movie; a rags-to-riches-to-rags roller-coaster ride that featured it all—bootlegging, conmen, and Al Capone. The story also included the much-suffering Touhy in a legendary case of injustice that still shocks to this day. Here's the tale.

Touhy started out an honest enough guy. After serving in the navy during World War I, he returned stateside again and put his all into trying to make an honest buck. But then the 1920s happened and everybody was raking in millions from bootlegging. By that time, Touhy gave in and jumped on the bandwagon. It wasn't long before he had his own gang.

Bootlegging in the Windy City was a pretty dangerous way to make a buck, and it wasn't long before Touhy came into direct contact with those illustrious mobsters Al Capone and Frank Nitti. Inevitably conflict broke out between the two gangs, and once again Chicago was a war zone.

### *JAKE THE BARBER*

Here's where the story really picks up speed. Like so many mobsters of the time, the Touhy gang went in for ransoming other hoods—it was a fast way to supplement the income and spread the dollars around. Capone, meanwhile, happened to know this guy—one John "Jake the Barber" Factor—who'd spent some time in England. While in Europe, Factor (who, by the way, was the half-brother of the famous Max Factor) had pulled off several truly sizzling scams, including one involving the British royals—a swindle that netted Factor millions. Another sting actually broke the bank at Monte Carlo.

On the run and in Chicago, Factor now sought protection from Al Capone. The authorities wanted to ship Factor back to England for trial, but he was far too wily for that to happen and he came up with a cunning plan. Factor would fake his own kidnapping and put the blame on the Touhy gang. This way he would be obliged to stay in the United States in order to testify at the trial, and Capone would get the Touhy gang out of his hair.

It was the old "two birds with one stone" gambit, and it paid off. Roger Touhy was framed and charged with snatching Jake Factor, a kidnapping that hadn't actually taken place. With a prosecuting judge snugly in his pocket, Capone made sure Touhy was found guilty and slammed with a heavy sentence. Poor Touhy got ninety-nine years for a make-believe felony.

So it was off to prison, but Touhy didn't give in to this piece of injustice. Instead, he rolled up his sleeves and began a frankly heroic campaign to win back his freedom, launching one appeal after another—all slapped down. Then, in 1942—and that's nine years already—Touhy began to get just a little desperate and he and several other inmates staged a bold prison break. For a brief but glorious time Touhy was actually on the outside and a free man.

It couldn't last, though. A few months after the break Touhy and the others were picked up and Touhy was thrown back into jail. This time the authorities tossed away the key—he got an additional 199 years tacked on to his sentence! Capone may have had something to do with that.

All of this only seemed to inspire Touhy to work that much harder. Finally, after latching onto a motivated and brilliant lawyer, he managed to dig up an honest judge and his case was reopened.

At long last, the much put-upon Touhy was exonerated of a crime he had not committed. But there was still that pesky business of the 199 years for the prison break. The obliging judge reduced that sentence down to three years and finally, in 1959, Roger Touhy was released from prison. It had been nearly twenty-six years.

Now that he was out, Touhy decided it was high time to settle a few scores. Capone by this time was very much dead, so there was not much Touhy could do about him. But there was still Factor, living like a king in Vegas. There were also other members of the Chicago Outfit who needed taking down a peg or two— Tony Accardo and Paul Ricca to name just two. Touhy and his inventive lawyer planned on launching a suit against all of them, demanding the staggering amount of three hundred million dollars. It wasn't likely such a suit would get anywhere, but it would certainly shine a very bright light on all the activities of Factor and the mob—and that was something the Outfit could not allow to happen.

So not even a month after he was released from prison and before his case went to court, Touhy was gunned down on the steps of his sister's house. He was only shot in the legs, but it was enough; he died a mere hour later from blood loss.

What a story, though. Check out Touhy's own book on his amazing life, *The Stolen Years*, to get the whole deal straight from the horse's mouth—up until the big death scene, of course.

# ALBERTO AGUECI
## OCTOBER 1961

### MESSAGE FROM THE BOSS

It used to be thought that the Mafia banned its members from dealing in drugs. This was not because drug money was beneath them, as some sources seem to insist. Really, nothing is beneath the mob. The actual reason was the effectiveness of the Federal Bureau of Narcotics (later the Drug Enforcement Administration) and the extremely long sentences associated with drug convictions. The thinking was that the longer a thug was in jail, the more likely he would be to flip and sing like a canary.

But there's just too much money to be made from narcotics, and where there's a buck, there's the mob. So although not officially sanctioned, many a mobster was able to make a fortune from drugs. They just had to do it on the sly. And any mafioso unfortunate enough to get caught dealing could consider himself on his own—there would be no protection from the boss. Basically, it would be the old kiss-off. And that's exactly what brothers Alberto and Vito Agueci got in the early 1960s.

The Agueci brothers had emigrated to Canada from Sicily and were part of a vast drug operation that stretched from Turkey through Sicily into France (the French Connection) and then into the United States via Canada. The brothers had set up shop in Toronto and belonged to Stefano "The Undertaker" Magaddino's family—a mob that operated out of Buffalo, but had tentacles that reached into Southern Ontario and Montreal. One of their partners in this racket was Joe Valachi, who later became part of Mafia legend as a high-profile informant.

Some time in the late 1950s the Feds began to get wind of the drug operation, and initiated a crack-down. Valachi was arrested in 1959, while the Agueci brothers went down in 1961. And with that, and for his own personal protection, mob boss Magaddino closed the door on them.

Alberto Agueci was enraged. He had fully believed he'd be bailed out by Magaddino and would receive the counsel of a top-notch lawyer. It was not to be. As reality slowly dawned on him, he began to lose his grip. Valachi later commented that he could tell Alberto was not going to do well in prison.

In desperation, Alberto's wife was forced to sell their lovely new Toronto home in order to bail the mafioso out. Once he was freed, Agueci headed straight to Buffalo and Magaddino.

### THE PRICE OF DEFIANCE

A mob boss who has been insulted is a dangerous enemy. The godfathers have their dignity and their standing within the Mafia to maintain. No insult can be ignored. Vengeance for any slight must be brutal and it must be swift. A message needs to be sent: "The boss will tolerate no disrespect."

Once Agueci had finished his tirade, and the smoke had settled a bit, Stefano "The Undertaker" Magaddino ordered two of his goons—Danny Sansanese and Freddie Randaccio—to take him out to a field somewhere and to deal with him. And, Magaddino told them, don't be gentle about it.

On November 3, 1961, Alberto Agueci's pitiful remains were found in a farmer's field. He had been unspeakably tortured over a number of days—his teeth were kicked in, his eyes were burned out with a blowtorch, and chunks of flesh had been removed from his legs while he was still alive. Finally, strangulation had ended his torment, and then his body had been set ablaze. There was nothing else to say. Magaddino had made himself heard.

Charles "Lucky" Luciano and his wife, Igea Lissoni, at their home in Naples after his deportation to Italy, in 1955.

# CHARLES "LUCKY" LUCIANO
## JANUARY 26, 1962

### THE MOB-FATHER

Charles (Salvatore) "Lucky" Luciano—he was the mob boss of all mob bosses. Luciano is what everyone envisions when they hear the word Mafia. There's a ubiquitous mug shot of Luciano that so epitomizes the mob and the man—that famous sneer, those steely eyes, one of them drooping a little because of a violent altercation he'd gotten into years before. That's the face of the Mafia.

A superb strategist, it was Luciano who removed the old Moustache Petes Joe Masseria and Salvatore Maranzano. And it was Luciano who truly organized crime, creating the Commission and the Syndicate—the latter being the organization that regulated the actions of all the mobs throughout the United States, regardless of ethnicity.

It's no understatement to say that Luciano was the greatest gangster in America (if the word "great" can be used for a gangster). And it was for precisely this reason that special prosecutor Thomas Dewey focused his energy on bringing him down. It's said that the charges were trumped-up, that a mob boss as elevated as Luciano would be well insulated from the actual criminal activities of his family. Nevertheless, charges of pandering were made and in 1936 Luciano was convicted, receiving from thirty to fifty years in prison.

## EXILE TO ITALY

Life in prison was certainly not tough for Luciano. He had tailored uniforms, specially cooked meals and his own radio on which he could listen to Abbott and Costello. He even had his own bodyguards and a pet bird. So proficient was Luciano that he was able to control his family from inside the prison, via his proxies, first Vito Genovese and then Frank Costello. But still, a prison is a prison.

By the beginning of World War II, however, the underworld had come up with a plan. The mob controlled the docks and shipping, and Luciano promised to ensure that the docks would be guarded and ships—both naval and commercial—would be protected from saboteurs. The mob was also to ensure that no strikes were to be staged for the duration, and Luciano himself was to convince his mob contacts in Italy to aid in the Allied invasion. It's not known how effective all of this actually turned out to be, but the plan worked as far as Luciano was concerned and his sentence was commuted. There was one condition, though—Luciano would be exiled to Italy.

So on February 10, 1946, Lucky Luciano headed to Naples to take up his residence in Italy. This exile hurt him very much, reportedly. Though he'd been born in Sicily, he considered himself American through and through.

In 1947 Luciano slowly tried to make his way back to the United States, but he only got as far as Cuba before his presence was flagged and he was forced to return to Italy. Once he was in Naples again, the Italian government cracked down on him, even curtailing his activities for several years. There was no way Luciano was getting out of the country.

Fast forward to 1962, when Luciano entered Naples International Airport. Apparently he was going to meet with film producer Martin Gosch, who wanted to make a movie of his life. As the pair walked to the parking lot, Luciano suddenly grasped his chest and fell to the ground. He had a bad heart and carried nitro pills, so the director hurriedly got some pills under his tongue. But it was too late—Luciano was dead.

The official ruling on the death of the mob boss of all mob bosses was heart failure. But there are those who claim that Luciano was poisoned, that the mob wanted to silence him before the movie could really get under way; or maybe the police had a hand in his death. Who can say? With the demise of Lucky Luciano, though, it was definitely the end of an era.

# ERNEST "THE HAWK" RUPOLO
## AUGUST 27, 1964

### MARKED FOR MURDER

Ernest "The Hawk" Rupolo had been a career criminal almost since the time he could walk. In a very early mug shot he looks only about twenty or so, and his mouth is twisted in a crooked smirk. Already, though, there is a patch over Rupolo's right eye. He had lost it in an earlier altercation and the offending bullet never exited his head; it remained there, lodged in his skull for the rest of his life, a terrible souvenir from a lifetime of violence.

A killer for hire, way back in the 1930s Rupolo had been involved in the contract that Vito Genovese had put out on Ferdinand "The Shadow" Boccia. It's not likely that Rupolo actually did kill Boccia, but he did know about the murder—all about it. Then, in 1944, he was picked up for the attempted murder of another mobster, Carl Sparacino. Facing a lengthy prison sentence, Rupolo decided to feed the authorities information about the Boccia killing; and his story would lead all the way to the top, to Vito Genovese of course.

No doubt about it, Rupolo was clearly a risk-taker. Possibly it was that bullet that was lodged in his brain. Maybe it had severed certain cerebral connections in his head that at one time would have given him access to common sense, or at least to the notion of self-preservation.

The accusation of Boccia's murder brought Genovese all the

way back from Italy so he could stand trial. But predictably, two of the key witnesses in the case passed away before they could testify, and Genovese was acquitted. Three years after this debacle, in 1949, Ernest Rupolo was back on the street and attempting—very vigorously—to make himself scarce.

One might imagine that Rupolo's life expectancy at this point would be pretty short, what with him being a stool pigeon and all. But Vito Genovese did not deal with him right away. In fact, years and years went by, and still the mob boss made no move against Rupolo. Maybe it was because Genovese had not been convicted of the Boccia murder, or maybe it was because he wanted Rupolo to suffer, to wriggle like a worm on a hook. Ultimately, his death did not fit into Genovese's plans, as of yet. So Rupolo was allowed to languish, waiting for the inevitable, as he made a meagre living from any small racket he could put together.

His number was finally up in August of 1964. Joe Valachi had just testified against the mob the year before, and this famous betrayal may have triggered something in Genovese, inspiring him to take revenge against all squealers, just on principle. They of course included Rupolo.

### CEMENT OVERSHOES

The body of Rupolo was found on August 27, 1964. The corpse was in a dreadful state. Bound at the hands, Rupolo had been stabbed and shot multiple times. With his feet encased in cement, his body was dumped into Jamaica Bay in New York.

His had been a hard-luck existence, but The Hawk really should have known that in the end there was no escaping his fate—even though it had been long ago, he'd still been marked for murder.

# JAMES "BUDDY" MCLEAN
## OCTOBER 31, 1965

### THE WINTER HILL GANG

It was known as the Irish Gang War—a mob battle that started in Boston, Massachusetts in 1961 and didn't end until 1967, when one of the mobs was completely wiped out and an estimated sixty hoods had been killed. And James "Buddy" McLean was the boss of the Winter Hill Gang—one of the most infamous and successful gangs in the United States.

McLean was a charismatic and respected leader, one who wasn't afraid to roll up his sleeves and get his hands dirty with the rest of his men. Though he had an angelic face, with "the map of Ireland" all over it as they say, McLean was a scrapper and had won the respect of Boston's Italian mob, headed by Raymond Patriarca.

The Winter Hill Gang was called an Irish mob, but it wasn't just Irish; the gang included other ethnicities as well, including Italian. One such Italian-American member was Alex Petricone. As an example of art imitating life, Petricone later became an actor. Look for him in *The Godfather*, acting under the name of Alex Rocco and playing the Bugsy Siegel-like character Moe Greene.

### *LABOUR DAY HOOTENANNY*

On Labour Day in 1961, friends of McLean were having a party with some of the McLaughlin Brothers, Boston's other notorious

"Irish" gang. Actually the gathering was a drunken bash, and during the bleary-eyed festivities, George McLaughlin made a pass at one of the other men's girlfriends. A beating ensued for McLaughlin, and he was dumped onto the lawn of the nearest hospital, more dead than alive.

George McLaughlin did survive, but his brother Bernie was furious. He went to McLean, demanding restitution. He wanted George's attackers rubbed out, and he wanted that pronto; but he needed McLean's assistance and go-ahead to do so. McLean tried to calm the situation; besides—he pointed out—George got what was coming to him, he should just walk it off.

This remark didn't sit too well with Bernie McLaughlin and after several attempts to get McLean to change his mind, he took action. A few nights later, while McLean and his wife were sitting in their living room, Mrs McLean saw some movement outside, around the family car. McLean went out, brandishing a gun, and chased two men off his property. He also found an explosive device attached to the bottom of his vehicle.

McLean had had enough and on October 31, 1961 McLean, aided by Petricone—the future Alex Rocco—took out Bernie McLaughlin as he left the Morning Glory Bar. McLean was arrested and there were dozens of witnesses, but astoundingly each one of them had suddenly no recollection of the event, and McLean did no time for the killing. All that could be pinned on him was illegal possession of a weapon, and for this, McLean got two years.

The first volleys had been fired in Boston's Irish Gang War. Over the next few years casualties were high, especially for the McLaughlin gang. Actually, the McLaughlins were all but collapsing and it was clear that their days as a significant mob force were coming to an end.

Allies of the McLaughlins took one last pot-shot however,

and on October 31, 1965, shortly after being released from prison, James "Buddy" McLean was shot down as he left the Tap Royal Bar.

The war would rage on for several more years, but despite this, the McLaughlins were pretty well dried up. And McLean's old gang? Though McLean was now dead, the Winter Hill Gang was just getting started.

# 5 THE SEVENTIES: TAKING CARE OF BUSINESS

**Notable Mafia hits of the decade include the murders of "Crazy" Joe Gallo, Sam "Momo" Giancana, Carmine "Lilo" Galante, and the disappearance of ex-Teamster leader Jimmy Hoffa.**

But the war against organized crime was about to get serious with the passing of the RICO Act in 1970, which gave law enforcement more effective tools with which to prosecute racketeers. Soon, more mafiosi than ever before were cutting deals in order to avoid lengthy prison sentences, as well as heavy fines. And of course, in the mob, there's only one way to treat a squealer.

# JOSEPH GALLO
## APRIL 7, 1972

### CRAZY JOE

Joseph Gallo was called "Crazy Joe", and with good reason. After being arrested in 1950 he had once been diagnosed with schizophrenia. But Gallo didn't let that condition keep him back, and he liked to view himself as a Renaissance man. During one lengthy prison stay, he availed himself of his extra leisure time to read Kafka, Dumas and Machiavelli. If it hadn't been for the war that Gallo started with mob boss Joseph Profaci, maybe he could really have made something of himself—he could have been a contender.

But at the very least Gallo had created a persona for himself, one that gave him a veneer of legitimacy—something he could use to his advantage. He was even a hit with the in-crowd of Greenwich Village—Jerry Orbach and Bob Dylan were Gallo fans.

Joe Gallo and his two brothers Larry and Albert were enforcers in the Profaci family, but they also ran some rackets of their own. In the early 1960s the greedy Joseph Profaci decided he wanted a higher cut from all his underlings' operations. Word was sent out and most of the family acquiesced—that is, all except for Joe Gallo and his brothers. In fact the Gallos decided to force the issue by kidnapping a number of high-ranking members of the Profaci family, demanding $100,000 for return of the captives. Profaci agreed, but it was the beginning of a war.

Score one was to the Gallos, but the next two scores definitely went to Profaci. In May of 1961 Profaci had Gallo operative Joseph Gioelli killed and in August of that same year Larry Gallo was attacked and nearly murdered. After these two strikes the Gallos stepped back and regrouped. Holed up in President Street, they kept a low profile for the next little while, surrounding themselves with a stockpile of weapons. But pretty soon money was getting tight, so Joe took some men and ventured forth to dig up a little of the green stuff. Putting the muscle on local businessmen, Joe managed to scrounge up some dough, but one of the shopkeepers had the temerity to go to the cops about the shakedown. As a result, Joe was sentenced to prison for up to fourteen years.

### THE TIMES THEY ARE A-CHANGIN'

By 1971 Joe was back on the street, but a lot had changed while he was in prison. Both Larry Gallo and Joseph Profaci were dead and the Profaci family was now run by Joseph Colombo. Hearing that Joe was out of jail, Colombo extended an olive branch, offering him one thousand dollars by way of a conciliatory gift. Gallo refused this gesture and demanded a hundred thousand instead.

As far as the mob was concerned, that was Joe Gallo's last chance; but Joe got to Colombo first. On June 28, 1971 Joseph Colombo was gunned down by a seemingly random shooter while speaking at an Italian Unity Day rally. Joe Colombo would remain in a coma for the rest of his life, and though no one could prove it, the mob knew exactly where the hit had come from.

The end came fast and furious. On April 7, 1972, Joe Gallo was shot several times while celebrating his forty-third birthday at Umberto's Clam House. Overturning a table, Gallo staggered out onto the street, where he crumpled to the ground. He died a short while later.

Whatever else Joe Gallo could have made of himself, admittedly it was pretty gutsy—and crazy—to start a mob war.

# DONALD KILLEEN
## MAY 13, 1972

### A NOSE FOR A STORY

This is the story of Donald Killeen. But it's also the story of the notorious James "Whitey" Bulger, since Killeen's story can't be told without reference to the double-dealing Bulger who offered up Killeen as payment in a deal with the devil (or the Winter Hill Gang in this case). This act of treachery completed, Bulger then embarked upon a bloody campaign that eventually won him complete control of Boston's underworld.

It could be said that everything began when Kenneth Killeen, Donald's younger brother, bit off the nose of Mickey Dwyer of the Mullen gang. As Dwyer was rushed to emergency, Killeen boss Donald picked up the nose, wrapped it in a napkin and sent it to the hospital for reattachment to the unfortunate Dwyer. But that nose episode was just an excuse for the start of yet another gang war in Boston.

In the 1960s and early '70s, the Killeens owned the southern part of Boston, termed Southie. The Mullens, though, there were plenty of them and really it was just a matter of time before the two gangs bumped noses. When the shooting began the city of Boston was knee deep in dead hoods.

Although the Killeens were the dominant gang, the Mullens were determined, and before long the Killeens found themselves backed into a corner. That's when Whitey Bulger, Donald Killeen's bodyguard, decided he needed to rethink his allegiance.

### TO KILL A KING

Going to Winter Hill leader Howie Winter, Bulger made it clear that he could put an end to the war—one that was costing numerous lives, not to mention money—by taking out his own boss, Donald Killeen. If Bulger could finish off Donald, he reasoned, then the rest of the Killeens would topple like dominoes. All that Bulger wanted in return was a position in Howie's mob. Winter could then absorb the remnants of the Killeens and the Mullens into his own gang. This way, everybody would win. Everybody except Donald, of course.

On May 13, 1972, Donald Killeen was at home, celebrating the fourth birthday of his young son. He went outside to fetch a toy train set that he'd hidden in the trunk of his car, but got fifteen bullets in the face instead. It's said that it was Whitey Bulger who pulled the trigger that day and then sped off in a waiting car.

With Donald Killeen gone, Howie Winter sued for peace with the Mullens and successfully took control of Boston's criminal world—but by 1979 Whitey Bulger had wrested leadership of the Winter Hill Gang from him, and the city was his.

# THOMAS EBOLI
## JULY 16, 1972

### THE SET-UP

When Tommy Eboli became head of the Genovese family in 1969 he must have thought that he had it made. After all, not only had the Genovese family once been the Luciano family, but it was still one of the most powerful mobs in the country. The only thing was, Eboli hadn't counted on Carlo Gambino, who had some ideas of his own concerning that particular branch of the Mafia.

Eboli had an interesting life, though. As well as being a made man and running rackets, he had also once been a fight manager—in fact he had handled the boxing career of future mob boss Vincent "The Chin" Gigante. One time, during a match, when he didn't like a decision the referee had made, Eboli climbed into the ring and physically attacked the man. Supposedly Eboli had arranged for the other boxer to take a dive, but the referee wasn't in on the fix.

Eboli paid his dues, slowly working his way up through the ranks until 1959 when his time finally came. That was the year that Vito Genovese was set up by the mob and sent to prison on a narcotics charge. This was Eboli's big chance, and he was promoted to the position of acting boss, along with Michele Miranda, Gerardo Catena and Philip Lombardo. Even though the role was shared, it gave Eboli a taste of power, and he found that he liked that taste very much.

So when Genovese died in prison and Eboli became the sole leader of the family he figured it was time to flex his muscles a bit. In 1972 he started a narcotics scheme and in order to finance this little venture, he borrowed a whopping sum of four million dollars from Carlo Gambino to get the ball rolling.

Trusting Gambino wasn't the smartest move Eboli could have made. Shortly after he had started to set things up, the police abruptly—and conveniently—got wind of the operation and swooped down. Eboli's cohort in the drug game, Louis Cirillo, was arrested and both the narcotics and the money that Eboli had borrowed were confiscated.

### TIME TO PAY UP

Now of course it was suddenly imperative that Carlo Gambino get his money back—every red cent of it. And naturally Eboli couldn't scrape the funds together. On July 16, 1972, Tommy Eboli exited his girlfriend's apartment at around one o'clock in the morning. As he entered his car a truck pulled up from nowhere and he was shot five times in the neck and head.

Now that Eboli was gone, Gambino lost no time with his next move and nominated a buddy of his—Frank Tieri—to the role of boss of the Genovese family. That was no surprise, since Gambino had been moving behind the scenes, placing trusted pals of his into positions of power for a while. Tommy Eboli had been just another pawn that had fallen to Carlo Gambino's gambit.

# SAM "MAD MAN" DESTEFANO
## APRIL 14, 1973

**MOB MONSTER**

Sam "Mad Man" DeStefano was a bona fide lunatic. In fact, he made "Crazy" Joe Gallo seem like a sea of calm. DeStefano was a loan-shark in Chicago and though he'd never become a "made man", he made buckets of money for the Chicago Outfit. He also put that money to use as a "fixer", greasing the wheels whenever anybody needed to get out of a jam. He had politicians in his pocket, and often bragged that he could get anybody off any charge—for a hefty fee, of course.

What DeStefano loved most was his "juice loan" operation. He'd lend money to anyone—political figures, or drug addicts from the street. He'd then charge a huge weekly interest on the loans (this was the "juicing" part—he'd squeeze his clients dry), and if they couldn't pay, he would have the opportunity of going to work. Truth be told DeStefano hoped and prayed that his clients wouldn't be able to make with the funds, especially the small fry. That way he could torture them to death.

DeStefano used to go out to the pig farms to watch the animals wallowing in the mud. He dreamed of the day when he would own his own farm so that he could feed his victims' chopped-up bodies to the swine. He also kept a soundproof torture chamber in his basement.

The list of DeStefano's unstable and violent actions goes on and on. He used to enjoy representing himself in court, where he would show up in his pyjamas, using a megaphone to get his point across. On the orders of mob boss Salvatore Giancana, he even executed one of his own brothers. He once shoved a gun into his wife's mouth and forced her to play an impromptu game of Russian roulette. And then there were the torture killings. DeStefano's life story reads like something from the history of Vlad the Impaler.

Usually the mob won't put up with such a noxious quantity as DeStefano—too much of a liability. Yet he was smart as well as crazy; his wealth and his usefulness as a fixer ensured he was around a lot longer than others might have been. Things changed when he killed Leo Foreman. Foreman was an underling of his and it was likely that he'd cooked the books and skimmed a little of DeStefano's money from the top of some racket or other. The consequences were predictably fatal.

Ten years passed before the cops were able to tie DeStefano to the case, but when they did he was finally brought in. It was said that he promised to sing in order to get a lighter sentence. In any case, DeStefano's usefulness to the mob suddenly came to an abrupt end and on April 14, 1973, he was executed. As a side note, one of Sam's killers was his remaining brother, Mario. What goes around comes around.

# RICHARD CAIN
## DECEMBER 20, 1973

## THE MOB AND JFK

Everyone who was old enough to understand the news at the time remembers the day that President John F. Kennedy was killed. It was like the moon landing, or the murder of John Lennon—an event that effectively stopped time for just a moment and seized the public consciousness.

Conspiracy theories galore exist around this event, but let's concentrate on only one of them—the involvement of the Mafia, and more specifically of Richard Cain, in the assassination of the president.

Cain (aka Richard Scalzetti) had been the mob's mole in the Chicago Police Department and with his espionage experience he assisted the Mafia in its plan with the CIA to bring down Cuban president Fidel Castro. Cain was of superior intelligence, spoke five languages and worked on training Cuban exiles for the Bay of Pigs Invasion. He was also said to be a crack marksman. All of these statements, save the latter, are verifiable facts.

Further, the bespectacled and innocuous-looking Cain had an extremely tight relationship with Mafia Don Sam Giancana himself. It has even been posited that Giancana was Cain's biological father. In short, Cain had the contacts, the know-how and the abilities to make him invaluable to the mob for this particular job.

So what was Cain's role in the death of the president? Well, the claim, supposedly from the mouth of Sam Giancana himself, was that Lee Harvey Oswald was not alone on that terrible day in 1963. Apparently Cain was there with him. What's more, it was actually Cain who fired the bullet that ended Kennedy's life, and not Oswald. The mob's motive in the killing, of course, was to halt the Senate's investigation into Mafia operations. In other words, the mob wanted to get the government off its back.

Ten years after the assassination, the Mafia decided they could do without Cain's services, and had him eliminated too. Shortly before he died, Cain apparently contacted FBI agent William F. Roemer and began to supply him with information regarding gambling operations in Chicago. It was Cain's plan to use Roemer in order to remove powerful gambling rivals and therefore take over the city's gambling scene himself. It was a typical Cain move, trying to play both sides.

If Cain was working with Roemer, there would be nothing to stop him from relaying everything he knew about the Mafia's involvement in the Castro Project (as the assassination attempt against the Cuban leader was termed) and the murder of President Kennedy. There was no way the mob could let Cain live.

### WHERE'S THE PACKAGE?

Cain was murdered inside Rose's Sandwich Shop in Chicago on December 20, 1973. That day masked gunmen entered the restaurant and forced everyone present up against the wall; then, asking where the package was, shot Cain—and only Cain—through the head several times before exiting. Supposedly before the killers left they took something from Cain's pocket, but what the item was no one can say. Possibly that move was only a ruse; we'll never know, because Cain's killers have never been identified. Sam Giancana was reportedly suitably upset when he heard about the murder of Richard Cain. It would have gone badly for the killers if he had ever caught up with them, whoever they may have been.

# ALEX "SHONDOR" BIRNS
## MARCH 29, 1975

### SAY IT WITH EXPLOSIVES

Taking care of business—in Cleveland they did it with bombs. Alex "Shondor" Birns, Cleveland's high-profile and violent Public Enemy Number One, knew this better than anyone. Birns was responsible for so many bombings that it would be hard to count them all.

Maybe the reason Birns felt the impulse to use bombs went way back to his childhood, during Prohibition. At that period, ordinary people got into bootlegging too, supplying local hoods with homemade rot-gut. One such ordinary person was Birns's own mother, Illon. One day, while Illon was tending to the family still, the makeshift apparatus exploded and she was killed, which must have devastated her young son.

By the time Birns was sixteen, he had started to fall in with the local hoods. A tough street fighter, he became a member of the Woodland Mob, before branching out on his own in the protection and numbers rackets. The money he earned was good, too, and gave Birns important contacts within the Cleveland Mafia.

Though he lived by his fists, Birns could be charming and affable when he wanted to be. He loved to drive expensive cars and dress in the latest fashions. He became great pals with the local press too, and would often shoot the breeze with them. But for all this, there was no denying how tough Birns was when the situation called for it. And of course, there were always his bombs.

### ENTER DANNY GREENE

Birns was very impressed by over-the-top Irish-American hood Danny Greene, who could bust it up with the best of them. In the early 1960s, Birn hired Greene as part of his mob and made use of Greene's fists (and guns) when needed. But hiring Greene turned out to be the worst move he ever made.

As the 1960s turned over into the 1970s, relations between Birns and Greene became somewhat strained. It didn't help that Birns felt Greene had reneged on a sizeable loan from him, one that he himself had borrowed from the Gambino family. So Birns put out a contract on Greene, and this being Cleveland, naturally one of the weapons of choice was a good old-fashioned bomb. It was too bad for Birns that Greene discovered the device before it could explode and decided to send it back directly where it had come from.

The end for Birns was truly terrible. On March 29, 1975, he left one of his favourite restaurants. Shortly after he got into his Lincoln and turned on the ignition, an explosion was heard that rocked the street, setting off car alarms. Glass rained down onto the pavement—the windows of nearby buildings had been blown out—and people came running from all directions. Birn himself had been blown through the roof of his car and severed in two; his upper body lay in one place, while his legs came down somewhere else. For all that, though, the tough old mobster was still alive for a few moments before his body shuddered and he faded into oblivion. Birns had died in the same manner he had inflicted on others.

# SAM GIANCANA
## JUNE 19, 1975

### THE CASTRO CONTRACT

Momo Salvatore Giancana (more familiarly known as Sam) was a real operator, rubbing elbows with Sinatra and the Kennedys and working on contracts to assassinate Fidel Castro. Giancana liked jet-setting and publicity and all the trappings that went with them. This high-profile existence didn't sit too well with the rest of the Chicago Outfit though, especially mob boss Anthony "Big Tuna" Accardo, who tended to play his cards close to the chest. To Accardo the only good publicity was no publicity. It was only a matter of time then before Accardo's patience with Giancana would wear out.

Giancana was the street boss for the Chicago Outfit. Having worked his way up through the ranks for years, he basically became the face of the Chicago mob in 1957. The real power at that time, though, lay in the hands of Accardo and Paul "The Waiter" Ricca, who controlled things from within the shadows, remaining well insulated.

This didn't mean that Giancana didn't have any authority, far from it. He was one of the most powerful mobsters in the country—a godfather. But on matters of great importance Giancana would defer to the decisions of people even more powerful—Ricca and Accardo. It was how the Outfit operated.

It's part of the Giancana legend that he'd fixed the votes in

Chicago during the Federal election of 1960, a strategy that gave John F. Kennedy the presidency that year. Then when the Kennedys didn't play ball as Giancana had expected—calling off the Federal investigation into organized crime—he came up with a supplementary arrangement, one that took place in Dallas, November 22, 1963. Who can say whether this is true? Countless books have been written on the assassination of JFK but no conclusive proof has ever been found.

But there are files in existence (the Family Jewels Documents) that detail how, as part of their Cuban Project, the CIA approached Giancana with the offer of a contract. The Agency wanted some assistance with the elimination of the Cuban president, Fidel Castro, and who better to take on a job like that than the Mafia?

Several attempts to poison the leader were made (apparently at the instigation of Giancana), but all in vain. Castro survived, and any further cracks at his life were kiboshed by the Cuban Missile Crisis.

### OFF TO MEXICO

Things changed rapidly for Giancana after this, though, and in 1965 he received a year in prison for contempt of court. On his release, he found it advisable to lie low for a while and headed to Mexico, where he made a fortune operating casinos. Unfortunately, he didn't see fit to share any of his gambling profits with the Outfit at this time, which was not a smart move.

The good times couldn't last forever and in 1974 Giancana was deported from Mexico and arrived back in Chicago again. What's more, he was also called to appear before a Senate Committee investigating the Castro contract that the CIA had put out.

By now Accardo had had enough. It doesn't matter who did it really, which friends of Giancana's were conscripted to pull the trigger. In the end, the go-ahead to kill him must have come from Accardo. So on June 19, 1975, Sam Giancana was assassinated while frying up some peppers and sausages in his basement.

# JIMMY HOFFA
## JULY 30, 1975

### WHO NEEDS BODYGUARDS?

July 30, 1975 may have been a summer day just like any other. No doubt children played in the park and people went about their business as they always did. That afternoon, Jimmy Hoffa, former president of the International Brotherhood of Teamsters union, headed to the Machus Red Fox Restaurant on Telegraph Road in Detroit. He was to meet up with Anthony Giacalone and Anthony Provenzano, two union men with heavy ties to organized crime. At least that was Hoffa's plan. Unfortunately neither Giacalone nor Provenzano showed up. At around 2:45 that afternoon a car did arrive at the restaurant, though, and Hoffa got into it. After that, Jimmy Hoffa was never seen again.

Theories abound as to what happened to Hoffa that day and why. Investigations have continued for years, with authorities digging through empty fields and into suburban residences, all with no result. Hoffa is gone, and his body will probably never be found, whether it's at the bottom of a lake somewhere or maybe encased in cement at Giants Stadium. We may never know just who assassinated Hoffa that day, but we can certainly surmise, and with a fair amount of accuracy, the reason why the job was done.

*Jimmy Hoffa in his D.C. office.*

## GET HOFFA

During Hoffa's time the unions meant big business to organized crime, and Hoffa definitely had his connections. Senator Bobby Kennedy and his "Get Hoffa" team had been after him for years, and in 1964 were finally able to convict him of jury tampering and bribery. A further successful charge was of skimming money from Teamster pension funds and funnelling it into the mob.

Hoffa of course appealed his conviction but was ultimately sent to prison in 1967, leaving trusted ally Frank Fitzsimmons as temporary Teamster president. Unfortunately for Hoffa, Fitzsimmons soon proved to be less of a friend, and began to put some distance between himself and the imprisoned union boss.

In 1971 things changed when Hoffa won a pardon from President Richard Nixon, on the stipulation that he resign and refrain from re-entering union business until 1980. This arrangement suited Fitzsimmons nicely, as well as the mob. In fact it has been speculated that the Mafia orchestrated the release of Hoffa in return for funds into the Nixon campaign (a move meant to keep the pro-Hoffa Teamsters pacified, something Fitzsimmons badly needed to do) so long as the ex-union leader remained out of labour politics. That last part, of course, was the important bit—Hoffa had to steer clear of the Teamsters. But the union was in Jimmy Hoffa's blood and for the rest of his life he vigorously attempted a return to Teamster leadership.

And that was the crux of the problem. Nobody wanted Hoffa back as union leader—not Fitzsimmons and not the mob. Certainly Hoffa had loaned out union money to the Mafia, but Fitzsimmons was now doing exactly the same thing, and much more generously. This was a cash cow that the Mafia was not about to let slip away. In the end, Fitzsimmons was a lot more malleable than the hard-nosed Hoffa had ever been.

193

And so on that day in July Hoffa, like Bo Weinberg, disappeared into history. The man who used to brag that he didn't need a bodyguard was declared legally dead in 1982. Today, Jimmy Hoffa's son James Hoffa is president of the Teamsters Union.

# JOE "THE ANIMAL" BARBOZA
## FEBRUARY 11, 1976

**PORTRAIT OF THE ARTIST AS A HIT-MAN**

He was known as "The Animal"—Joe "The Animal" Barboza. But that name doesn't come anywhere near describing the knot of contradictions that was Joe Barboza. A hit-man who was responsible for some twenty or thirty murders, he was also an intelligent self-taught individual who was a trained chef, wrote poetry and painted pictures (apparently very good ones, too).

Barboza became involved in organized crime after making some contacts in prison during the 1950s. He freelanced in the New England area, offering his services to the Winter Hill mob and Rhode Island's La Cosa Nostra family, the Patriarcas. A hulking ex-heavyweight boxer, he made a very imposing impression with his barrel chest, huge forearms and massive head. Barboza both looked and behaved exactly like what he was—an ex-boxer and a mobster. He got his nickname "The Animal" after taking a bite out of some thug's ear during an altercation in a bar. Yet paradoxically Barboza was also said to love animals and children, and would sometimes take the neighbourhood kids to the zoo.

In 1966 the Mafia decided to remove their support from the combustible Barboza. In October of that year, Joe was picked up on weapons charges, his bail set at a hefty one hundred thousand dollars. There was no way that Barboza's crew had that kind of money, so they set up a collection fund, hitting local hoods for contributions. Shortly after they'd managed to put together fifty-nine thousand, Barboza's men were hit and the bail money was scooped up by members of the Patriarca family. When he heard what had happened, Barboza understood exactly what that meant—the mob had turned its back on him.

While awaiting trial for the weapons charge, Barboza was approached by Federal Agent H. Paul Rico, who hoped to convince him to testify against the Mafia. After much soul-searching, Barboza came to the conclusion that he would co-operate—it was time to do to the mob exactly what they had done to him.

### PRISON POET

It was while he was in prison that Barboza penned his poems outlining Mafia treachery in such works as "Boston Gang War", "The Mafia Double Crosses", and "The Gang War Ends". The Animal's anguish found its voice.

Barboza found another voice as well when he implicated mobsters Raymond Patriarca, Henry Tameleo and other members of the Patriarca family in just about every crime that had occurred in the last few years. Barboza's agenda was to cause as much damage to the mob as he possibly could and he wasn't too choosy how he went about it. He even accused mob men of a murder that he himself had committed.

Agent Rico had promised all sorts of protection to Barboza for his testimony—he was one of the first to enter the Witness Protection Program—but after he got what he was after, Rico reneged and Barboza was left to fend for himself. There was no way he could have much time left after all that and the end came on February 11, 1976. As he was leaving the apartment of a friend, Joe Barboza was shot four times at close range and died instantly.

*John Roselli arrives, under tight security, to testify before the Senate Select Committee on Intelligence in Washington, D.C.*

# "HANDSOME" JOHNNY ROSELLI
## SUMMER, 1976

### THAT DAY IN DALLAS

Johnny Roselli was thought to be in on the CIA plan to murder Cuban dictator Fidel Castro (that one's a definite "yes") and the assassination of President John F. Kennedy (there's still a lot of debate over that one). It seems that the Mafia was really busy in the 1960s and Roselli was at the forefront.

Roselli had good looks ("Handsome" Johnny), with an impressive mane of silver hair, immaculately tailored suits and two dimples that appeared when he flashed his winning smile. He was the perfect face to be the Outfit's man in Hollywood, then in Vegas, skimming money from the casinos.

Apparently Roselli was also the perfect contact in the plot to kill JFK too. If you take into account all the conspiracy theories, Dallas was lousy with assassins that day in November of 1963 when Kennedy was shot. According to some, not only was Lee Harvey Oswald there, in the Texas School Book Depository, but also Richard Cain (either with or without Oswald), Charles Nicoletti of the Outfit and various members of the CIA and the FBI.

And then there was Handsome Johnny Roselli. According to various writers, Johnny was either on his way to Dallas in order to abort the assassination or he was actually one of the shooters, aiming from his position down a sewer drain. That sounds like a rather difficult shot. But aside from flights of fancy, many believe there is compelling evidence to suggest mob involvement in the assassination of Kennedy, and to implicate Roselli as well.

The fact is that Roselli did not need to be one of the shooters to be involved. A figure as highly placed in the mob as he was wouldn't have pulled a trigger anyway. At that level nobody sends you to do a job like this, you send somebody else.

What it all comes down to is that the mob was feeling a lot of heat from Senator Bobby Kennedy (JFK's brother) in his zealous crusade against organized crime. To the Mafia, pressure from the government meant a loss of revenue, and put the boys at the top—Sam Giancana of Chicago and Santo Trafficante of Florida in this case—in compromised positions. Those things alone were more than enough to make the mob take action.

In the 1970s, all of this started to unravel and Roselli was in the thick of it. He appeared twice in front of Senate Committees with regard to the Castro and Kennedy affairs, on September 22, 1975 and April 23, 1976 respectively. And during all this, Roselli was not pleading the Fifth and keeping his mouth firmly shut, the way a mafioso should do—he was being rather forthcoming with his testimony.

### THE BODY IN THE BAY

Roselli was expected to testify in front of the United States Senate Select Committee once more, but his body surfaced in Florida's Dumfoundling Bay. That was August 9, 1976. He had been shot and strangled, then stuffed into a barrel and tossed into the water. His legs had been cut off so he would fit into the drum; newspapers of the day even wrote that Roselli may have been still alive when he was thrown into the bay, though today we know this to be incorrect. Roselli had done some talking, but once again the Mafia had had the last word.

# RICHARD J. CASTUCCI
## DECEMBER 29, 1976

### MURDER AND MISDIRECTION

Sam Giancana is reputed to have said that the mob and the CIA were basically two sides of the same coin. Whether or not that's true, there have undoubtedly been CIA agents—and FBI agents for that matter—who were more interested in pursuing their own agendas than upholding the law. In fact some agents have gone so far as to actively assist the mob.

Take Agent John "Zip" Connolly of the FBI, for instance, who accepted bribes, falsified records and became involved in racketeering—and that's just for starters. Actually, Connolly went a whole lot further than any of that would suggest. He was cheek by jowl with Boston mobsters James "Whitey" Bulger and his buddy, Stephen "The Rifleman" Flemmi and consistently tipped them off on relevant FBI proceedings. It could almost be said that Connolly was a mole for Bulger.

That's where Richard Castucci enters the picture. He was no angel; a member of the Patriarca family, he owned several notorious clubs and ran high stakes gambling games. But for all that, Castucci, a family man, was nowhere near as bad as Whitey Bulger or Stephen Flemmi.

Some time around 1970 Castucci got himself into financial trouble, owing large sums to loan sharks and to the Patriarcas.

So, as a solution to his financial woes, Castucci became an informer to the FBI in exchange for a pay-off.

### THE WINTER HILL MOB

Castucci got hold of some hot information regarding Bulger's gang, the Winter Hill mob; he had discovered where two wanted members of that gang, Joseph McDonald and James Sims, were hiding out. He passed his knowledge on to the FBI, as was part of his agreement. Connolly of course found out about the tip-off and forwarded the information on to Bulger.

Predictably, the end for Castucci was unpleasant. On December 29, 1976, Bulger, Flemmi and another Winter Hill member—John Martorano—lured Castucci to a secure location and put a bullet in his head. They then rolled the body into a sleeping bag and hid it in the trunk of Castucci's own car. When he was finally found his body had frozen.

The FBI immediately suspected Bulger and Flemmi of the murder and initiated an investigation, but Connolly put a stop to this and immediately began to deflect the investigation away from his Winter Hill pals and toward the Patriarca family. Because of this cover-up, the FBI did not pursue Whitey Bulger for the murder of John Castucci.

The truth, however, was clamouring to be heard. When Stephen Flemmi was at last arrested in 1995 he decided that his best defence was to do a little deflecting of his own. Flemmi put the finger on Connolly and revealed the whole dirty business— Bulger and Connolly's arrangement.

Today, Bulger, Flemmi and Connolly are all behind bars. As a side note, in 2009, the family of Richard Castucci received a cash settlement of over six million dollars from the Federal Government because of Agent John Connolly's failure to do his duty.

# FRANK "BOMP" BOMPENSIERO
## FEBRUARY 10, 1977

### TALES FOR THE FBI

Was Frank "Bomp" Bompensiero a slick mobster and FBI informant or simply an inept fall guy? It's a good question. Certainly Bompensiero was around for a long time, something that is worthy of note for a Mafia man. Also, when Frank Dragna ran the Los Angeles mob, Bompensiero was important enough to be the boss of the San Diego crew.

But, significantly, Bompensiero was demoted to the rank of mere soldier after Dragna's death in 1956, when Frank DeSimone took over the mob. DeSimone and Bompensiero just didn't see eye to eye. Bompensiero had been a prolific hit-man for years, specializing in something called the Italian rope trick. In this, the victim is greeted with a hug by someone he considers a friend. While he is occupied, two other mobsters come up on either side of him and wrap a rope around his neck. Bompensiero wasn't trusted, or even liked, by many people. He did have one pal, though—Jimmy Fratianno. The two had met in prison, and Fratianno relied on him for many years.

Naturally, after Bompensiero was demoted he became dissatisfied with his position in the LA mob, and asked for a transfer to Chicago. Unfortunately his request was denied, so it was understandable that he began to chafe a bit in his new, diminished role. An unhappy mobster is a dangerous mobster, and by 1967 Bompensiero had become an informant for the FBI.

His arrangement with the agency went on for a number of years, and for a while Bompensiero was able to get his own back on the sly. But a deal like that couldn't last forever, and some time in the early 1970s Dominic Brooklier, the new boss of the LA mob, began to grow suspicious of Bompensiero.

A contract was put out on Bompensiero, but the wily mobster was very hard to pin down. He knew every trick in the book, having used most of them himself. Around the same time though, his usefulness to the FBI had begun to run dry. The fickle agency had now set its sights on Bompensiero's old friend Jimmy Fratianno. Mob boss Brooklier had just been sent to prison and in his absence Fratianno had become a very important man—acting boss of the LA mob.

### THE STING
So the FBI decided it was time to sell Bompensiero down the river in a trade-off that would net them Fratianno. In 1977 Bompensiero came into possession of information regarding a couple of small-time pornographers who were ripe for a shakedown. He passed the information on to Fratianno, who sent over some enforcers to pay the guys a visit. The film distributors were actually undercover FBI agents who proceeded to lower the boom on the hired muscle. After Fratianno questioned Bompensiero, and didn't like what he heard, the penny dropped—he realized that Bompensiero was an informer.

On February 10, 1977 Frank Bompensiero was shot down as he made a few calls in a telephone booth in Pacific Beach. There's plenty of irony in this story, though, at least as far as Fratianno is concerned. Some time before Bompensiero's death, Brooklier was released from prison and took up his old role of LA mob boss. Fratianno, in his turn, was demoted—and he became the next FBI informant, one of the highest ranking in the history of the mob. So much for *omertà*, the oath of silence.

# DANNY GREENE
## OCTOBER 6, 1977

### THE CELTIC MOBSTER

An Irish-American mobster who gave away green pens, had a green office with a green rug, flew the Irish flag outside his home and named his gang the Celtic Club, Danny Greene saw himself as a modern-day Celtic warrior, a Brian Boru or Cuchulain from legend. And together with another independent working outside the purview of the mob, John Nardi, he went to war with the Cleveland Mafia and blew the city apart.

To some in Greene's home turf of Collinwood on the east side of Cleveland, he was a hero, the Collinwood Robin Hood, who would distribute turkeys and hams on Christmas and Easter and never let a local family go hungry. But that was only one side of the complicated Greene. He was also a union leader who embezzled money from the Longshoreman Union's coffers, was a known FBI informant and tried to take control of the Cleveland rackets, no matter what the cost.

The local Cosa Nostra was not giving up without a fight, but for long time they didn't seem to be equal to the task of eliminating him. Every hitman they sent after Greene came back having failed, if they came back at all. There was an aura about the guy, a certain mystique, and it seemed to be growing. Greene didn't avoid the mob—he publicly taunted them, daring them to bring it on.

206

## ALTERCATION WITH THE HELL'S ANGELS

The story is told of how Greene confronted a branch of the Hell's Angels as they tried to set up shop in his neighbourhood. He entered the dilapidated hangout with a lit stick of dynamite by way of illustration. If the bike gang caused any trouble, Greene promised, he would blow them to kingdom come—hideout and all. He then removed the fuse from the dynamite, and walked away.

Every day that Greene survived, every moment that he went against the status quo—blowing up his enemies as he did so—the prestige of the Cleveland family suffered. The situation became so dire that families from other parts of the country offered to send over help if the Cleveland mob could not tend to its own backyard. Greene just seemed to be invincible.

But he wasn't, of course. Finally in May of 1977 Greene's partner John Nardi was killed—by a bomb, naturally enough. Then on October 6 of that year Greene met his own end. Exiting a dentist's office, he got into his car just as the automobile next to his exploded. Losing his legs and an arm, he died instantly.

However, the death of Danny Greene initiated an investigation that brought down the top players of Cleveland's Mafia and eventually put a dent in La Cosa Nostra nationwide. Though Greene was no longer around to see it, he and Nardi had beaten the mob.

# JOHNNY MENDELL
## FEBRUARY, 1978

### MENDELL'S FATAL MISTAKE

In Chicago, the Outfit called the shots. And from 1947 to 1992 Anthony "Joe Batters" Accardo—aka "Big Tuna"—definitely ran the Outfit. Anybody who dared lock horns with Accardo was asking for trouble. Johnny Mendell, on the other hand, was just a burglar—a very good one, but still, no match for Accardo. Unfortunately that's not the way Mendell saw it.

On December 21, 1977, Johnny Mendell and his collaborators robbed Harry Levinson's jewellery store on North Clark Street. The job was beautiful and smooth; the thieves got in and out leaving no evidence behind. By the time they were finished the crew had nearly cleaned out Levinson's shop, omitting only the famous "Idol's Eye Diamond", a beautiful blue pear-shaped gem. But other than missing out on that prize, Mendell and his gang were probably feeling pretty good about the burglary. Once they'd fenced the goods, they could look forward to a happy and prosperous New Year.

Unfortunately Mendell hadn't realized that Levinson was an old pal of Tony Accardo. Concluding he wouldn't get much help from the police, Levinson contacted his old friend. If anyone were able to recover the jewels, it would be the boss of Chicago's underworld, the Big Tuna himself. Accardo agreed and put the word out on the street—the goods better turn up, and fast.

Apparently the thieves obliged, because the jewels were silently and quickly returned. And that should have been the end of it. After all, Mendell had been playing it fast and loose by not checking with the Outfit in the first place. If he had, he would have known that Levinson's was off limits and saved himself a lot of grief. Apparently, though, Mendell played by his own rules and not the Outfit's.

Mendell was not pleased with the way things turned out. He had put a lot of time and money into that job and now had nothing to show for it. Something was owing to him, and he knew just where to get it.

## THE RUTHLESS DON

In early January of 1978 Accardo and his wife had left the Windy City for a vacation in California, and while they were away, Mendell took the opportunity to break into their house—the personal home of the godfather of the Chicago Mafia.

When Accardo heard the news he was apoplectic. He was a ruthless Mafia Don, not someone to mess with; his vengeance for this slight was swift and it was brutal. One by one the Mendell crew dropped. Some had been stabbed, others garrotted, all had turned up stuffed into the trunks of cars. Mendell, whose body was found on February 20, 1978, had been tortured before he'd been killed.

In the end at least nine people were murdered, allegedly on Accardo's orders, two of them having nothing to do with the burglary at all. It was Mendell's fatal mistake, and it was one that he would never have the opportunity to repeat.

Joseph Colombo with members of his family and members of the Italian-American Civil Rights League leaving St. Patrick's Cathedral after praying for an end to alleged harassment by the FBI's strike force.

# JOSEPH COLOMBO
## MAY 22, 1978

### STOLEN YEARS

After he was shot, Joseph Colombo lay in a semi-coma for nearly seven years. As life passed by without him, all he could do was raise one or two of his fingers in a feeble attempt at communication—the only thing left to him. It's said that he could recognize faces, but nothing more.

But before that, Colombo had been a godfather and the boss of the family that still bears his name. In charge for nearly ten years, Colombo was one of the youngest bosses leading a mob at that time. And today, some people still praise him for being forward-thinking, for trying to bring the Mafia into more legitimate enterprises, and for activism in civil rights.

Italian-American unity was Colombo's passion. He wanted to wipe Italian stereotypes away—stereotypes of violence and the mob that led, he believed, to targeting by the FBI and the police. To that end he created the Italian-American Civil Rights League, an organization he hoped would foster a feeling of unity within the country. Despite his position as mob boss, Colombo made real efforts with the IACRL, allying the organization with the Jewish Defence League in a quest for tolerance.

But despite Colombo's denial of the existence of La Cosa Nostra (and they all denied it back then) and his activism, he had been in the mob for years and as a Don himself oversaw money-making operations that included smuggling, counter-feiting and extortion, to name just a few. At least, though, Colombo put some of his ill-gotten gains to good use.

## THE GALLO WAR CONTINUES

Even after Colombo took over the family, there was still that lingering war that had begun in the early 1960s with the old boss and Crazy Joe Gallo and his crew. And Gallo wasn't one to let things go. When he got out of prison in 1971, he was still looking to settle the score with the Colombo family, and as usual with Gallo, he took his grievance straight to the top.

It happened at an IACRL rally in June of 1971. The scene was festive, music was in the air and Colombo was just about to climb the podium to give a speech. That's when Jerome Johnson made his way to the front of the crowd, masquerading as a member of the press. With a clear view of Colombo, apparently to take pictures, Johnson whipped out a pistol and shot him in the head and neck. The Don fell, the scene erupted into pande-monium and in all the confusion someone shot and killed Johnson. Colombo was rushed to the hospital, but the damage had been done; he remained in a semi-comatose state for the rest of his life.

No one was ever arrested for the shooting of Colombo or Johnson, but the authorities had a pretty good idea who arranged the hit. So did the mob, and ten months later Joe Gallo was shot inside Umberto's Clam House. He died within minutes—an ending that was very much faster than the one for Joseph Colombo.

# THOMAS "TWO-GUN TOMMY" DESIMONE
## DECEMBER 1978/JANUARY 1979

### A LOVE FOR VIOLENCE
In the movie *Goodfellas*, the character Tommy DeVito is based on Thomas "Two-Gun Tommy" DeSimone. Actor Joe Pesci won an Academy Award for that role. Mobster Henry Hill has been quoted as saying that the actor's performance was dead on, and he would know.

DeSimone was a pal of gangster James "Gentleman Jim" Burke and a member of the Lucchese family. Described as a psychopath even by those who knew and admired him, DeSimone once killed a man in the street—an innocent stranger—just to prove how tough he was.

Tommy DeSimone's brother Anthony had been executed for being an informant and DeSimone expended a lot of energy trying to live this dishonour down. Anyway, he loved violence for its own sake. He used to take great pleasure in breaking noses and teeth, or shooting off kneecaps with the guns that he used to carry around in paper bags.

### THE LUFTHANSA HEIST
Nobody ever knew what was going to set off DeSimone next. Things got so bad that he once killed a "made man"—William

"Billy Bats" Bentvena—for some off-hand remark Bentvena had made. Killing a made man without permission was not done in Mafia circles. DeSimone tried to dispose of the body, stuffing it in a trunk and hauling it off somewhere for burial. Bentvena was not quite dead yet, and began pounding on the trunk for release. This didn't deter DeSimone, who stopped the car, and together with Jimmy the Gent, he proceeded to finish the job.

DeSimone's biggest claim to fame, though, was his involvement in the Lufthansa Heist of 1978, a robbery that netted Burke's crew around six million dollars in cash and jewellery. It was a spectacular job, beautifully planned and beautifully executed. And the loot has never been recovered.

One thing went wrong with the heist, however. Immediately following the job, driver Parnell Edwards decided to get high and flop at his girlfriend's pad instead of disposing of the getaway van like he was supposed to. The van was found in a no-parking zone and the FBI immediately tried to tie the case to the Burke crew. Edwards had to be removed from the picture.

It was up to DeSimone to deal with Edwards, a job that he carried out several days after the heist. In fact Edwards was only the first to die because of his involvement in the Lufthansa robbery. Burke managed to dispose of a total of ten people associated with that robbery, which of course meant more money for him.

With his latest murder under his belt DeSimone was feeling pretty good. He'd been promised that with this job he'd become a made man. So some time in December of 1978 or January of 1979, DeSimone was brought to an unknown location where the induction ceremony was supposedly to take place. Of course, there was no ceremony, and Tommy "Two-Gun" DeSimone disappeared without a trace.

No one really knows who killed DeSimone, but the prevailing theory is that the Gambino family was responsible because of that Billy Bats Bentvena incident all those years ago.

# HARVEY "CHRIS" ROSENBERG
## MAY 11, 1979

### COLOMBIAN REVENGE

Harvey Rosenberg, aka Chris Rosenberg, aka Chris DeMeo, was a member of the DeMeo crew, a branch of the Gambino family. In fact, he was so tight with the crew's boss, Roy DeMeo, that he was practically a son to the mobster as well as his second-in-command.

In the 1970s, cocaine, hashish and Quaaludes all flowed freely, and represented big money. Rosenberg was heavily into drug trafficking, and in 1979 had the opportunity to score a big haul from a loan shark in Florida—one Charles Padnick who, through a Cuban intermediate, had connections with a Colombian drug cartel. As a general rule, Colombian drug lords are not the kind of people to mess with, but Rosenberg thought he'd pull a fast one.

Padnick, the Cuban and several representatives of the Colombian cartel flew to New York to seal the deal. But as soon as the two groups met, Rosenberg and some others of the DeMeo crew plugged the opposition full of holes. They then took the drugs and the money. When news of the double-cross reached the Colombians they demanded prompt restitution and they held the Gambino family responsible. In fact, the Colombians promised war unless Rosenberg was executed. The drug lords also demanded that the killing be sufficiently high profile that it would hit the papers. That way they could be sure the job had actually been done.

The Gambinos agreed. After all, the stunt Rosenberg pulled was bad for business, making it seem as if the Mafia could not be trusted. No one wanted that.

The order came down—Rosenberg had to go, and Roy DeMeo had to do it. This was bad news for DeMeo, who put off the killing and waited, in the hope that maybe things would blow over.

### DEATH OF THE PROTÉGÉ

They didn't, of course, and the Colombians became impatient. They sent over some enforcers to stir things up if Rosenberg wasn't executed soon. DeMeo got so twitchy that he accidentally killed a young college student who was selling vacuums door to door, thinking he might be a Colombian enforcer. After that, Gambino boss Big Paulie Castellano said time was up, Rosenberg had to go.

So on May 11, 1979, when Rosenberg met with the rest of the DeMeo crew as usual, the meeting took a slightly different turn than expected. He was shot five times in the head and his body was left in an abandoned car by the side of the road. Then the car was blasted with bullets, ensuring that the murder would be sensational enough to hit the papers. It's said that Roy DeMeo was terribly distraught at having to kill his protégé, but pragmatism won the day.

*The body of Carmine Galante is covered by New York police detectives at a Brooklyn restaurant on the 12th of July, 1979.*

# CARMINE "LILO" GALANTE
## JULY 12, 1979

### THE FRENCH CONNECTION

When Carmine "Lilo" Galante was sent to prison in 1931, a psychological evaluation of the time concluded the mobster had an IQ of only 90, the mental capacity of a fourteen year-old, and that he was emotionally "dull". How such a profoundly inaccurate judgement could have been reached defies the imagination. With a career in the Mafia that spanned fifty-four years, Galante was one of the most effective hit-men ever in operation. His coordination and virtual control of the Mafia's narcotics operations showed a superb mind with an aptitude for organization, and his flagrant takeover attempt of the Bonanno family is a classic example of Mafia realpolitik.

During the 1950s, "Lilo"—which is slang for "cigar" in Italian, and a nod to Galante's habit of perpetually smoking them—was heavily involved in the Bonanno family's drug affairs. In fact, drugs were his focus for much of his Mafia life, and he oversaw international operations that spanned from Sicily through Marseille (the French Connection), Canada and the United States.

In 1962, however, Galante was sent to prison for twenty years. This proved to be no set-back for him. He retained all of his narcotics contacts, keeping the lines of communication open and allowing him to remain a powerful force in the drug world.

## *THE BANANA WAR*

During Galante's incarceration, big things were happening in the Bonanno family. Joseph Bonanno and Profaci family boss Joseph Magliocco were scheming to eradicate the bosses of the other families in a bid to take over the Commission. The fall-out from this attempted coup brought down the wrath of the Mafia and caused a wide division within the Bonanno family itself, splitting the gang in two. The conflict is referred to as the Banana War, and ultimately it led to Joe Bonanno's forced retirement and exile from the mob.

The removal of Bonanno led to a power vacuum within the Bonannos which was eventually filled by Philip Rastelli, who assumed leadership in 1974. But he didn't have much time to wield power. In 1976 Rastelli was sent to prison.

With the leadership of the Bonanno family still precarious, the stage was set when Galante was finally released from prison in January of 1974. Without skipping a beat, he set in motion a series of plans that he had been refining for years and that were designed to give him a monopoly over the Mafia's drug operations as well as control of the Bonanno family.

Using mobsters and bodyguards—known as Zips—that he had imported from Sicily, Galante began to muscle out the other families from the drug business, concentrating specifically on the Gambino family, towards whom he held a great animosity. The Sicilian Zips were reputedly loyal and unquestioning and they owed their elevated status to Galante.

After Bonanno boss Rastelli was sent to prison, Galante declared himself de facto Don of the Bonanno family. With all the millions that Galante was raking in from his international drug operations (money that was not shared with the other families) and his Cossack-like Zips surrounding him, Galante carved out an unparalleled position for himself.

This would be his undoing. By 1979 the other families, and Rastelli from within his prison cell, voted for Galante's elimination. On July 12, 1979, Carmine "Lilo" Galante entered Joe and Mary's Restaurant in Brooklyn. After a pleasant meal with the restaurant's owner—Giuseppe Turano, who was a cousin of his—Galante went outside with Giuseppe to enjoy the sunshine on the restaurant's patio. They were shortly joined by mob capo Leonard Coppola and two Zips.

Just as Galante was about to light up one of his ubiquitous cigars, three men in ski masks burst their way out to the patio and began firing. Galante was blown backwards onto the cement, and Turano and Coppola went next. Pictures of the gruesome scene—legendary now in mob folklore—show Galante lying with his head propped against a curb, his right hand clutching a lighter, while his left hand lies limply across his chest. A cigar—a lilo—is clamped in his mouth. Interestingly, the two Zips were unharmed in the attack—a sign that they probably had inside information.

Though he would not be paroled until 1983, Joseph Rastelli was now able to secure his position as boss of the Bonanno family. Carmine "Lilo" Galante, the mafioso that even other mafiosi feared, had been neutralized.

# 6 THE EIGHTIES: THE LAW FIGHTS BACK

**The 1980s were a difficult time for the Mafia. First, there was the battle in Philadelphia caused by the assassination of not one but two Dons, Angelo Bruno and Philip Testa. Later on, there was the Scarfo/Riccobene conflict which seemed to send Philadelphia back to the 1930s in terms of open warfare.**

Big things were happening in New York, too, with the Donnie Brasco affair that led to the execution of Dominick Napolitano and the takeover of the Gambino family by the Teflon Don, John Gotti. All in all, it was no cakewalk to be a card-carrying member of the mob.

# ANGELO BRUNO
## MARCH 21, 1980

### THE GENTLE DON

Angelo Bruno was known as the Gentle Don, but though he certainly did prefer compromise over violence, he would use force when the situation called for it. He was, after all, a Mafia godfather. The truth was that fortunately for Bruno, the Philadelphia family was removed from the battles that had over the years afflicted the families of New York. The Philadelphia mob was aloof, and could afford to be low key.

The precise reasons for Bruno's downfall remain unclear, but the most likely cause is simply greed. For a long time, Bruno required that his family adhere to the Cosa Nostra ban on dealing in narcotics. Possibly for Bruno this was a matter of honour as well as practicality. Philadelphia was clean—at least as far as the mob and drugs were concerned. And while Bruno was in charge, his house was in order.

But some time in the late 1970s Bruno received a visit from Carlo Gambino, boss of one of New York's most powerful families. He wanted Bruno's sanction for the Gambinos to traffic in Philadelphia. This request was for courtesy's sake only, since Gambino was far more powerful than Bruno. But the set-up would not be without its rewards and of course, Bruno would receive a cut of the profits. You don't say no to Carlo Gambino, even if you are Angelo Bruno. The Gentle Don had no choice, and he was forced to acquiesce.

This got some of the Philly mob grumbling—if Bruno could make money from drugs, why couldn't they? In fact, a few of them—Bruno's consigliere Antonio Caponigro in particular—took the argument to its logical conclusion and began to consider ways of removing the Don from the picture altogether.

### IMMORTALIZED IN DEATH

It's another of those iconic mob murder photos—Angelo Bruno, sitting in the rear seat of his car, his head thrust back and smeared with blood, his mouth gaping open as if forever crying out at the instant of death. The end for Angelo Bruno came on March 21, 1980, and even the other mob lords were taken aback.

No matter what support Caponigro (aka "Tony Bananas") may have believed he'd receive, Bruno's assassination had in no way been sanctioned by the Commission and in the mob, there is only one punishment for murdering a boss without consent. The rest of Caponigro's part in this story writes itself then: shortly after Bruno's death, Caponigro was summoned to New York to meet with the bosses of the other families. His body was later found folded in the trunk of his car. Dollar bills had been stuffed into his mouth (and elsewhere), signifying his greed.

The Gentle Don was gone. The death of Angelo Bruno initiated a period of infighting and incompetence in Philadelphia that eventually saw the demise of that family.

# PHILIP TESTA
## MARCH 15, 1981

## OPEN SEASON ON GODFATHERS

The body of slain mob boss Angelo Bruno had hardly cooled when his underboss, Philip "The Chicken Man" Testa, became head of the Philadelphia mob. Not that Testa had had anything to do with the demise of Bruno—that had been the work of Antonio Caponigro, who'd paid a terrible price for his transgression. This didn't stop Testa from benefiting from the death of "Gentle Don" Bruno, of course.

Testa's tenure as godfather should have been a successful one. He intended to take the best of Bruno's regime—the late mobster's sense of tradition and honour—and add some new, badly needed improvements, in his view. Testa planned on opening up Philadelphia to mob-sanctioned drug trafficking, something that had been banned under the old boss, as well as inducting some fresh blood into the fold. As soon as Testa grasped the reins he brought in a whole flock of fledgling mobsters who took the oath, pricked their fingers and became fully-fledged mafiosi.

As many as nine men—Salvatore "Chuckie" Merlino, Frank Narducci Junior, and Testa's son, Salvatore, among them—received their buttons (became "made men") one night in 1980 or '81, in an initiation ceremony that featured the traditional burning of saints' cards as part of the ritual and undoubtedly ended in unbridled celebration.

Testa had done everything right, in other words. Everything should have worked. But blood had been spilled and the smell of death was in the air. There was now no holding back the dogs of war.

### ANOTHER ONE BITES THE DUST
Greed—it was the same thing that had inspired the murder of Bruno. Peter Casella, Testa's underboss, didn't want what Testa was selling—the drug opportunities (Casella had been in trafficking himself anyway), the new mobsters in the club. Casella wanted more.

Once again a member of the Philadelphia mob committed murder without the full permission of the Commission. The story goes that Casella whipped up a bomb that sported twenty sticks of dynamite and had finishing nails embedded in it. When Testa came home on the morning of March 15, 1981, the device was detonated as soon as he stepped foot on his porch and opened the front door. The explosion was devastating and could be felt nearly three miles away. Despite being blown straight into his kitchen, Testa was still alive, at least initially; he died several hours later, after being rushed to the hospital. It hadn't even been a year since the death of "Gentle Don" Bruno.

Another mob boss had been murdered in the city; that made two in less than a year. But the war was just getting started in Philadelphia.

# ALPHONSE INDELICATO, DOMINICK TRINCHERA, PHILIP GIACCONE
## MAY 5, 1981

## THE THREE CAPOS

Even though mob usurper Carmine "Lilo" Galante had been dealt with in July of 1979—his body crumpled on the back patio of Joe and Mary's Restaurant in Brooklyn, a burning cigar still in his mouth—Bonanno boss Philip Rastelli was really not much better off than before. He was, after all, still in prison. And what's more, certain members of the family were not at all happy with the new division of power, the most vocal of these being capo-regime Alphonse Indelicato. One thing was clear to Rastelli—the battle for the Bonanno family was not yet over.

Rastelli was relying heavily on his two allies, Dominick "Sonny Black" Napolitano and Joseph Massino, to run things for him while he was still in jail. Napolitano and Massino were extremely loyal to Rastelli. It was a good thing they were, too, because Indelicato had allies of his own.

They were known as the Three Capos—Alphonse "Sonny Red" Indelicato, Dominick "Big Trin" Trinchera and Philip "Phil Lucky" Giaccone—and they were significant players. Indelicato realized that with Rastelli languishing in prison and with the Machiavellian Galante out of the way, leadership of the Bonanno family was still very unstable. If he acted now, what was there to stop him from becoming head of the Bonannos himself? It was worth a try.

The only problem was, any move Indelicato could make would undoubtedly start another Bonanno war, and nobody wanted that. Not him. Not Rastelli. And not the Commission. Talks of peace were attempted and with the intervention of the Commission, the Three Capos were convinced to bury the hatchet, at least for a while. But the concord didn't last, and it wasn't long before the Three Capos were voicing their dissatisfaction again.

Napolitano and Massino had to act quickly. A meeting was called at the Embassy Terrace Catering Hall. And that's when it all went down.

### THE RED FACTION

It happened on May 5, 1981. Indelicato, Trinchera and Giaccone arrived at the hall, but Indelicato didn't like the way things looked. He'd taken the precaution of scattering his men in different hideouts throughout the city. That way, if things blew up, the rest of his faction—the Red Faction—would not be wiped out all at once.

It didn't really matter though, because once the door closed on the Embassy Terrace basement, and the Three Capos were trapped in the killing room, all hell fatally and forcefully broke loose. Nine men closed in and, pulling out weapons, blasted into the Capos. Big Trin was shot in his ample belly. He was followed to the floor by Giaccone. Indelicato tried to run, but was shot down before he could make it to the door. Smoke filled the room, and blood tattooed the floor. The Three Capos were gone and the Bonanno family could be at peace again—at least until the next murder was decreed.

Among the shooters that day was Montreal mobster Vito Rizzuto. The Montreal family was on the rise.

# DOMINICK NAPOLITANO
## AUGUST 17, 1981

### THE DONNIE BRASCO AFFAIR

The last thoughts of a marked man—they're not often known. And when they are, it's usually evident they've been reduced to one single, desperate plea—the desire for life. But Dominick Napolitano was different, a cut above the usual mobster. We know this because of Joseph D. Pistone, referred to by the Mafia as Donnie Brasco.

Pistone was a Fed, an FBI agent who'd worked on infiltrating the mob for six years. When Pistone—Brasco—was introduced to Bonanno capo Napolitano, the two became fast friends. Napolitano had interests outside the "club" and he and Brasco would often pal around together, going out for coffee, or playing tennis. Sometimes they'd talk as they fed Napolitano's valuable homing pigeons.

But all the time that he was getting closer to the Mafia and to Napolitano, Pistone was compiling evidence that would indict more than 200 mobsters, and convict more than 100 of them.

In 1981 Napolitano decided it was time to promote Brasco and he gave him the contract on Bruno Indelicato. With the job completed, Napolitano promised, Brasco would finally become a "made man". At that point the FBI pulled the plug on the operation. It was a no-win situation. Pistone, of course, could not commit the murder; but to refuse the contract would mean his own death. You can't say no to the mob. Donnie Brasco, then, quietly disappeared.

## THE CHANCE TO ESCAPE

Now that the game was up, the Feds approached the capo. If news of the Brasco deception were to reach the Bonannos—which it inevitably would—Napolitano's life wouldn't be worth a plug nickel. But if Napolitano were to become an informant the government could offer him protection.

And this is when Napolitano—Mafia man though he was—showed his true mettle. He refused to break *omertà*. Though his life could now be counted in mere days, Napolitano would not betray the mob. Nor would he run.

On August 17, 1981, Napolitano was summoned to a meeting. It was "the" meeting, and he knew that it was. Handing his keys, his ring and the care of his beloved pigeons into the hands of the bartender of the Motion Lounge, an establishment that he owned, Napolitano phoned his girlfriend to say goodbye, telling her that all this wasn't Brasco's fault—he was just doing his job. After that he headed to the home of Bonanno associate Ron Filocomo. Once he arrived, he was pushed down a staircase into the basement, then the shooting began. Reportedly the first bullet missed him, and Napolitano demanded that the killers fire again, and this time make a good job of it. The door to the basement closed.

When Napolitano's body was found in Staten Island, his hands had been cut off—a symbol that he had welcomed an infiltrator into the Mafia. But Dominick Napolitano went to his death with his back straight, his shoulders squared and bearing no ill-will to his friend Donnie Brasco.

# ROY DEMEO
## JANUARY 10, 1983

### THE DEMEO CREW

Some mobsters turn out to be stand-up guys in the end. Take Dominick Napolitano, for instance, who had a personal code of honour that he would not deviate from, no matter what the cost. Roy DeMeo, on the other hand, was a different kettle of fish. Roy—nasty and brutish—and the DeMeo crew built up a reputation in the Gambino family for a number of things, including narcotics and car theft. But the main focus of the DeMeo crew, its real *raison d'être*, was murder. To sum up, DeMeo just liked to kill.

The specialty of this band was something called the Gemini Method, named after the club where the crew used to hang out—the Gemini Lounge. The Gemini Method involved knives, saws and plastic garbage bags deployed by a crew as efficient, and coldblooded, as a factory. It's hard to track how many people they had done away with because the bodies were so difficult to find. Estimates range anywhere from 75 to 200.

DeMeo's greatest wish was to become a "made man", but mob boss Big Paulie Castellano, who viewed himself more as a businessman than a hood, didn't want to give credence to the thuggish and murderous DeMeo and his crew. Then in 1977 DeMeo brokered a fantastic deal, letting the Gambino family in on some of the lucrative rackets that the Irish mob, the Westies, were running in Hell's Kitchen. After this, even Castellano had to admit that DeMeo was an earner, and he opened the books.

But it was murder that DeMeo loved best, and after a while he began to freelance, taking contracts outside the mob, just so he could keep his hand in. Inevitably then, before long, the crew began to devour its own. In 1978 and '79, Roy had DeMeo crew members Danny Grillo and Chris Rosenberg murdered, for either real or imagined infractions. It must be said, though, that supposedly DeMeo wept after killing his protégé Rosenberg.

### TOO MANY BODIES

But things couldn't go on like this forever. Some time around 1982, the police were finally able to connect the dots regarding the stolen car ring they'd been investigating and the mysterious dismembered corpses that kept popping up. DeMeo was beginning to draw a lot of unwanted attention—an unforgiveable crime in the Mafia—and had to go. Yet at first Castellano had a hard time finding anybody willing to take the contract—DeMeo and his crew were just too feared.

By now DeMeo, who was getting rather paranoid, began to consider faking his own death and going on the lam. But the Gambinos beat him to the punch. Finally on January 20, 1983, the body of Roy DeMeo was found stuffed into the trunk of his car. It's rumoured that it was members of his own crew that finally picked up the contract on Roy. After all, it was what they did best.

# JASPER CAMPISE & JOHN GATTUSO
## JULY 1983

### GET ETO!

The hit on Ken Eto was going to be the job that gave Johnny Gattuso promotion to "made man". It shouldn't have been too hard. Just lure Eto to a quiet parking lot, wait until he parks the car, place a gun next to his skull, then it would be over. Only it didn't happen that way and though Campise and Gattuso thought they'd planned every detail, somehow after all the smoke had cleared, Eto was still standing upright. More than that, he was now ratting everyone out, and big time.

Ken Eto was a Japanese-American in the Chicago Outfit. His was not the usual ethnicity, but he was a good earner, bringing in millions. He'd worked for the Outfit for years too, since 1949 running a bolita game—a numbers racket—and lining the pockets of Vincent Solano, Eto's boss and boss of the whole North Side.

Eto was true-blue too, a reliable goodfella who could always be counted on to do his job, keep his mouth shut and generally toe the line. The last thing Eto ever wanted to do was to rat out his pals—it just wasn't part of his makeup. It was too bad Solano didn't understand that.

Everything started to unravel some time in the early 1980s when the Feds began to clamp down on Eto's bolita game. That's when Solano started getting nervous. The mob boss just didn't realize that he had nothing to worry about when it came to Eto. The best thing to do, Solano felt, was to get rid of the problem altogether. No doubt about it, it was time to get Eto.

Of course, Eto knew that it was coming; he knew he had no choice, and decided to go the way they wanted him to.

The contract eventually made its way to Jasper Campise and John Gattuso, the Abbott and Costello of Chicago's underworld. But maybe Eto had been born under a lucky star or something; in any case, it just wasn't his time to go. Campise and Gattuso had everything worked out so nicely. They'd even packed the bullets themselves so they'd be more difficult to trace. And that's how everything fell apart—there just wasn't enough oomph in those slugs.

Picture it. There they are, all three of them, sitting in the car, Eto waiting for them to blow his head off, playing the game; Campise relaxing in the back seat, talking pleasantly about the dinner they were going to have, trying to keep Eto's suspicions under wraps. Gattuso raises his gun and blam—three times. There's blood everywhere and Eto slumps over sideways in the car. Campise and Gattuso get out of the car and head out into the night, confident of a job well done.

Much to his surprise and delight, Eto found that he was still alive. Pulling himself out of the car, he staggered to a drugstore, where he called for an ambulance.

### SINGING A NEW SONG

Of course, if Eto wasn't going to flip for the Feds before, he was certainly going to do it now. He told the FBI about everything—crooked cops, old robberies and unsolved murders. He also told a lot about Solano. Eto even told stuff about the mob that hadn't happened yet. But it was all gold. Ken Eto proved to be a most reliable informant.

And Campise and Gattuso, of course their days were numbered. The latter was going to be "made" for the Eto job. Instead he ended up in the trunk of an abandoned car, curled up next to his buddy Campise. The pair had been missing for a few days when they were found on July 14, 1983. It was the foul odour emanating from the vehicle that prompted a local resident to call the police.

Eto spent the rest of his days in Georgia, living under an assumed name. Ken Eto—or Joe Tanaka as he came to be called—lived to the ripe old age of eighty-four and died of natural causes.

# ROBERT RICCOBENE
## DECEMBER 6, 1983

### THE SCARFO/RICCOBENE CONFLICT

The war in Philadelphia continued. Mob bosses Angelo Bruno and Phil Testa had met their spectacular ends in 1980 and '81 respectively. Control of the Philadelphia family had been awarded to Nicodemo Scarfo, through a deal he'd brokered with the Gambino and Genovese families, for partial interest in the gambling mecca of Atlantic City.

Not everyone was pleased with this state of affairs, however. Chief among Scarfo's detractors were the Riccobene brothers— Harry, Mario and Robert—since Scarfo was expecting the Riccobenes to pay tribute, something they'd never had to do before. It seems that under Bruno and then Testa, the Riccobenes had held special status, been independents and as such, hadn't had to share their wealth. Now, with Scarfo calling the shots, all of that was about to change. Harry, naturally enough, had other ideas.

"Little Nicky" Scarfo was a ruthless operator. Whereas Don Bruno would use murder as a last resort, for Scarfo violence was always the opening move. It was no surprise, then, when Scarfo decided it was time for Harry to go. He just didn't expect the Riccobenes to fight back.

### BLOODY TURF WAR

It was open war in Philadelphia, the kind of knock-down, shoot-'em-up bloodbath that used to explode in Chicago during the 1920s and '30s. Gunmen drove through the streets and bodies were dropping everywhere. Once, while Harry was making a call from a phone booth, the Scarfo faction happened by and shot him five times. That wasn't enough to take out Harry, though—the 70-year-old managed to knock the gun from his assailant's hand and was still standing after the incident.

Failed attempts like this were getting under Scarfo's skin, and he ordered the boys to step it up a bit. Though they managed to hold their own for quite a while, the Riccobenes couldn't stand up to the rest of the Philly Family. It didn't help that by 1983 not only Scarfo but Harry and Mario Riccobene were in prison. With two top players gone, the Riccobenes weren't able to hold out much longer.

It was the last volley in the battle for Philadelphia. On December 6, 1983, Robert Riccobene was returning home from shopping with his mother. As the pair stepped out of their car, Scarfo's men opened fire. Robert turned to run, but didn't get very far and fell dead as he tried to hop a fence. He had been murdered right in front of his mother, a supposed breach of Mafia rules, which shows far things had gotten out of hand.

The Riccobenes had been subdued, and Little Nicky Scarfo was busy carrying out business from his prison cell. In fact, Nicodemo Scarfo was just getting started.

# CESARE BONVENTRE
## APRIL 16, 1984

### THE SICILIAN

Cesare Bonventre was a "Zip", one of those native Sicilians brought over to America by Carmine "Lilo" Galante. In fact Bonventre was one of the bodyguards who'd been sitting with Galante on that hot day in June when his boss was splattered all over the sticky back patio of Joe and Mary's restaurant in Brooklyn. Bonventre, along with Baldassare Amato, should have been looking out for Galante that day, even taking a bullet for the mob boss. Galante trusted his Zips when he wouldn't trust anybody else. The truth is, though, there's ample evidence to suggest that both Amato and Bonventre were in on the hit. Galante should have known—in the Mafia, there can be no trust.

The Zips probably got their name because of the fast way they spoke the Sicilian dialect, so fast that the American mafioso could hardly understand them—the words just zipped by. The term was not meant as a compliment. The North American mob did not like the Zips; they were too violent, too secretive and not trustworthy. The antipathy was mutual.

### THE PIZZA CONNECTION

Cesare Bonventre was a high earner in the drug trade. No doubt learning a lot from Galante, he was heavily involved in heroin trafficking. A scheme called the Pizza Connection smuggled drugs into North America on a billion-dollar, international scale. Once the narcotics reached the United States, they would be passed through various pizza parlours, where the stuff could be distributed and money could be laundered—hence the name Pizza Connection.

By 1984, the FBI had begun to catch on to the Pizza Connection and were issuing indictments like Halloween candy. By this time, Bonventre also had other problems. He had drawn the ire of Bonanno family acting boss Joseph Massino, who viewed him as a threat. With two strikes against him—a possible pending trial and Massino—Bonventre could not be long for this world.

It happened on April 16, 1983. Bonventre had been picked up by Salvatore Vitale and Louis Attanasio for a meeting that was to take place at a glue factory, which boded ill. Once the group pulled up to the factory Attanasio unloaded two bullets into Bonventre's head. It's said that Bonventre was almost 6ft 9in in height (though this may be an exaggeration), and his nickname was "The Tall Guy". Two bullets were not enough to fell him, and he made a grab for the steering wheel. When the car careened to a stop, Bonventre tried to drag himself across the factory floor in a bid for safety.

But the game was up, of course. Attanasio stood coolly over Bonventre's struggling form and finished him off with two more shots to the head.

# SALVATORE TESTA
## SEPTEMBER 14, 1984

**THE KISS OF DEATH**

If there was anyone that Salvatore Testa should have been able to trust it was his godfather, *the* Godfather—Nicodemo Scarfo. Testa had known Scarfo all his life and looked on him as a father. He should have had nothing to fear from the man, but nobody was safe with Scarfo.

"Salvie" Testa was the son of Philip "Chicken Man" Testa, that same Chicken Man who had run the Philly family after the death of Don Angelo Bruno, and who was later himself murdered through the use of a nail bomb. It's said Salvatore was a Mafia blueblood, that he'd been born and bred for the life. They called him the Crown Prince of the Philly Mob. Standing over 6ft tall and darkly handsome, he looked the part.

After the death of Salvie Testa's father, Scarfo took over the Philadelphia family and a new regime—one of violence, intimidation and fear—was initiated. Testa became a capo in this new regime, standing right beside Scarfo. After all, he was the son of a late mob boss, and Scarfo's godson.

When Scarfo went to war with the Riccobene brothers, Testa was there, dishing it out with the rest of them. In fact Testa was a specific target of the Riccobenes, and received several dangerous wounds in that war. He recovered, but with scars that were marks of his loyalty to Little Nicky Scarfo.

It wasn't all one way, though; Testa drove fear into the hearts of the Riccobenes and was never as happy as when he was finally able to take revenge on the men who had murdered his beloved father Philip. In all, it's said he was responsible for at least eighteen deaths.

### ON THE RISE

As the 1980s rolled on, Testa was everywhere and the media were beginning to take notice of the handsome and charismatic gangster. In fact, the press were starting to refer to the mob prince as a rising star in the Mafia.

Little Nicky Scarfo was taking notice too and he didn't like what he saw. Testa was becoming too popular and getting awfully close to the top. The jealous and unstable Scarfo was beginning to view him as more of a threat than a godson. Uneasy lies the head that wears the crown.

Some time in 1984, then, Little Nicky Scarfo ordered the hit on a man who had been like flesh and blood to him—Salvatore Testa. At a Mafia funeral, Testa was singled out and given the kiss of death.

On September 14, 1984, Testa was lured by his best friend to the Too Sweet candy store, ostensibly for a meeting. Once inside, he received two shots to the back of his head and died immediately.

During the early 1980s the Philly family existed in an atmosphere of paranoia and treachery, thanks to Scarfo's mismanagement of the mob. Over the next few years, Nicodemo Scarfo would be tried on a number of charges—including Salvatore Testa's murder—and as a result, will now probably spend the rest of his life in prison. Among those who testified against him were members of Scarfo's own Philly family—mob men who no longer felt any loyalty for the man who had had his own godson murdered.

Paul Castellano leaves Federal Court after posting $2 million.

# PAUL "BIG PAULIE" CASTELLANO
## DECEMBER 16, 1985

### THE DON GOES DOWN

Paul Castellano was not the most popular Mafia Don ever to come down the pike. He was somewhat standoffish, aloof. In fact, there was a large chasm that existed between Castellano and the average soldier. The regular street thug felt it. What's more, some "made men" in the Gambino family felt that Castellano should never have become boss at all. One of those mafiosi was John Gotti.

In the late 1970s through the early 1980s, the Gambino family was split into two factions—not a good thing at any time. One faction was loyal to Castellano, while the other felt more loyalty to Aniello Dellacroce. The latter had been in the Mafia for years, had been Carlo Gambino's underboss, and should have become the boss when Gambino died; at least that's what the Dellacroce faction felt. But Gambino wanted the leadership to stay in the family, so he bequeathed the top spot of the Gambinos to his brother-in-law, Castellano. Dellacroce himself was fine with this, at least outwardly. He was an old hardliner, and if the big boss wanted Castellano, then Castellano it was.

Castellano was another one of those bosses who banned dealing in narcotics yet lined their own pockets with drug money.

Gotti was a member of the Dellacroce faction, and he was dealing in drugs—hard. And the ambitious Gotti thought he'd make a much better successor to Gambino than Castellano.

Things simmered for a while, with neither Castellano nor Gotti really doing anything while Dellacroce was still alive. The old mobster seemed to be keeping a lid on things. But on December 2, 1985 Dellacroce passed away from cancer, and the situation came to a head pretty fast. With Dellacroce gone, there was nothing to stop Castellano from using Gotti's defiance of the narcotics ban to whack Gotti and his whole crew. The only thing was, Gotti saw it coming and got there first.

### DEATH ON THE MENU
On the evening of December 16, 1985, Big Paulie Castellano arrived at the famous and pricey Spark's Steak House in Manhattan. He was there to attend one of those supper meetings that mobsters favour. As he was exiting his Lincoln—along with his chauffer and underboss, Thomas Bilotti—three men dressed in white trenchcoats and wearing black Russian hats stepped out of the milling crowd. Pulling out revolvers, the men shot Paulie six times, then plugged Bilotti full of lead.

It was a smooth, smooth hit and afterward Gotti and Sammy "The Bull" Gravano drove by the bodies to make sure the job had been done. Gotti must have been pleased with what he saw—there was nothing now to stop him from becoming boss of the Gambinos.

# FRANK DECICCO
## APRIL 13, 1986

### REVENGE FOR THE DON

Big Paulie Castellano had been bumped off right in front of Spark's Steak House in Manhattan. His body lay partially outside his Lincoln, his feet stretching out onto the frigid New York sidewalk, while his head rested just inside the car. What an iconic mob picture.

John Gotti was now the boss of the Gambino family, possibly the most powerful of the Five Families, while the position of underboss went to Frank DeCicco, a mastermind of the Castellano murder. The Don was dead, long live the Don.

DeCicco was intelligent and capable, a solid guy who could be trusted. Gotti relied on him and gave him control of the so-called White Collar crimes, the rackets that Castellano had preferred over the street jobs such as robbery and narcotics.

But the positions of Gotti and DeCicco were far from secure. Though Castellano was no more, Gotti had not received permission from the Commission for the job, and in the Mafia, that's a problem. As Antonio Caponigro found out when he killed Don Angelo Bruno in New Jersey, only the Commission can authorize a hit on a boss. The Commission was not pleased with what just went down in New York.

## VINCENT "THE CHIN" GIGANTE

Genovese boss Vincent Gigante (aka "The Oddfather") was most enraged. Gigante practically controlled the Commission at the time, and did not like the breach of Mafia protocol that Gotti had committed. Besides, he had been a tried and true buddy of Castellano's, making a lot of money with the Gambino Don. Gigante went to Lucchese boss Victor Amuso for support, and the two of them decreed that both Gotti and DeCicco had to go. The plan was to use explosives to make the hit look like the work of the Zips.

Amuso outsourced the job and hired Westies member Herbert Pate to do the deed. The time came on April 13, 1986, when both Gotti and DeCicco were to attend a meeting at the Veterans & Friends Social Club. As Pate strolled through the parking lot of the establishment, two bags of groceries in hand, he pretended to drop one of the bags. When he knelt down to pick up the groceries, Pate affixed an explosive device under DeCicco's car. Then he went off to wait.

Some time later, DeCicco exited the club and headed to his car. He was accompanied by Lucchese soldier Frank Bellino, who coincidentally resembled Gotti to a certain extent. Pate, of course, mistook Bellino for Gotti, and detonated the device. The parking lot exploded. Bellino only lost a couple of toes, but DeCicco was blown to bits. When Sammy "The Bull" Gravano came racing out of the club to see what happened, he found that DeCicco was literally in pieces and beyond help.

The kicker was that Gotti wasn't even at the meeting that day. He had planned to attend, but then had to cancel. Gigante and Amuso would have to be satisfied with the death of DeCicco for the time being—Gotti had been spared. The violence between the three Families, though, was not yet over.

# VLADIMIR REZNIKOV
## JUNE 13, 1986

### LUCCHESE PROTECTION

In the early to mid-1980s, the Russian Mafia—or Mafiya—was just beginning to get a foothold in the United States. One place that was rich in Soviet emigrés was Brighton Beach in Brooklyn. That's where Russian mob boss Marat Balagula set up shop and ran such rackets as credit card scams and gasoline bootlegging. He was making a sizeable profit for himself and his crew, and owned a beautiful mansion as well as the Odessa Restaurant on Brighton Beach Avenue. But all that money flowing into Balagula's coffers was a red flag (or gold flag) to the Colombo family, and before long the Colombos began to shake down members of Balagula's gang.

There was only one thing he could do, Balagula concluded—in the end it would be best to try to swim with the Mafia sharks rather than against them. So he put out feelers and asked for assistance from Christopher Furnari, consigliere of the Lucchese family.

Furnari agreed to provide protection to Balagula—for a small fee, of course. As long as the Russian allied himself with the Lucchese family, they would make sure that nothing happened to him and his rackets. The price for this service would be insignificant—just a tax of two cents per gallon of gas sold. These profits could then be divided between the Five Families and everyone would be happy. It was a stroke of genius and the gas racket became a goldmine for the Mafia.

### RUSSIAN STREET THUG

This is where Vladimir Reznikov comes in. Reznikov heard about Balagula's deal with the Italians and decided he wanted in on the gasoline pie. Driving past Balagula's office one day, Reznikov pulled out a rifle and shot the place up. That was just his opening salvo.

Now that he'd gained Balagula's attention, Reznikov became more brazen and stormed into the Odessa restaurant. Waving a Beretta in Balagula's face, Reznikov demanded the payment of $600,000. If Balagula refused to pay, Reznikov would make short—and brutal—work of him. Balagula agreed, and promised to get the cash; but then as Reznikov left the restaurant, Balagula collapsed to the floor, struck down by a heart attack.

Resting at his home, Balagula called in his mob contacts. Now was the time for the Mafia to earn its keep. As requested, Balagula handed over a picture of Reznikov as well as a description of his car. Wheels had started to turn.

On June 13, 1986, Reznikov returned to the Odessa with his hands open. When he found out Balagula wasn't there, he stormed out of the restaurant, got into his car and prepared to drive off. He didn't get very far, for a gunman stepped up to his vehicle and fired through the window. Reznikov attempted to get out through the passenger side and pull out a revolver, but one final bullet put a swift end to him.

Word went out onto the street pretty quick after that—mess with Balagula, and you're dead.

# ANTHONY SPILOTRO
## JUNE 14, 1986

### ON THE FAST TRACK

There's one rule of thumb every mafioso knows—if the mob says you have to go, then you have to go. The only thing you can do is pray it's fast and quick. That way you can close your eyes, take it on the chin and go out like a champ. Tony Spilotro and his brother Michael, though, didn't go fast at all.

For a long time Tony Spilotro—aka "The Ant"—seemed to be on the fast track. For a good ten years, he really looked like the favoured son of the Chicago Outfit. "Made" at the tender age of twenty-five, Spilotro could do no wrong and in 1963 he was given the lucrative racket of bookmaking in Chicago's Northwest Side. But the best for Spilotro was still to come and as his career progressed, the press began to speculate that he was well on his way to being the next big boss for the Outfit.

Spilotro had a pretty cold-blooded reputation. After all, he had cut his mob teeth as part of the crew of Sam "Mad Man" DeStefano, who liked to go in for torture killings when he was lucky enough to get the go-ahead on a hit. Spilotro allegedly took part in a lot of those murders in the early years, including the savage death of mobster William "Action" Jackson in 1961, a torture killing that went on for days.

## THINGS TURN BAD

As early as 1971 Spilotro, who was all of thirty-three at the time, was given the plumb prize of overseeing the mob's operations in Vegas. With his base in that gambling mecca, Spilotro successfully ran the Outfit's casino-skimming racket, a narcotics enterprise and a burglary ring, and expanded his territory into Arizona.

But Spilotro was his own worst enemy and as far as his gang was concerned he wasn't making any friends. A ruthless boss, Spilotro seemed to use the same iron fist technique when managing his crew. As a result a total of five of Spilotro's men became informants at the close of the 1970s and into the 1980s. The Outfit was not impressed.

Things got much worse, though. For his skimming endeavours in Vegas, Spilotro was blacklisted from the casinos in 1979. Also that year he was arrested for murder and was accused of defrauding the Teamsters. In 1981 he dealt with a racketeering charge and in 1983 another murder charge. This kind of attention is what the mob hates most—it has the tendency to bring down the heat on the big bosses, and the smart ones like to stay in the shadows.

But the final nail in Spilotro's coffin was hammered home when a number of top mob leaders, including Chicago's street boss Joseph Aiuppa, were convicted of casino-skimming based on testimony from Spilotro's men. As a result, profits from Vegas slowed to a trickle and boss Aiuppa got twenty-eight years. All this was more than enough to seal Spilotro's fate.

On June 14, 1986 Anthony "The Ant" Spilotro and his brother Michael were called to a meeting at a Bensenville, Illinois home. The brothers were told that Michael was going to be made, but they both knew better. Once there Tony and Michael were brutally beaten, then strangled. Their battered bodies were later found buried in an Illinois cornfield. So it can't be said that Tony and Michael Spilotro went fast, but maybe they went out like champs.

# MICHAEL "THE BAT" DEBATT
## NOVEMBER 2, 1987

### THE HAUNTED HIT

So many hits over the years, so many goodfellas who have paid the price. Perhaps some mafiosi are not at all happy with the way they shuffled off this mortal coil and are still hanging around, trying to come to grips with what happened to them.

Take the case of Michael DeBatt, who was a mob casualty, one of the many who have been whacked over the years. This is not to say DeBatt was completely innocent himself, but it's highly probable that he got in over his head.

DeBatt was a friend of Sammy "The Bull" Gravano, and also a member of Gravano's Gambino family crew. Gravano had at one time been very good to DeBatt, helping his family deal with loan-shark debts after the death of his father, and more or less taking the young lad under his wing. According to Gravano, who later famously became one of the biggest mob informers ever, DeBatt took part in the murder of Frank Fiala. But that's just Gravano's testimony. No murder charges against DeBatt were ever laid.

DeBatt was doing okay for a while. He had a wife and child, a nice home and a restaurant—Tali's—that was helping to pay off some of his father's debt, as well as giving DeBatt a new start. So what went wrong?

Unfortunately for DeBatt, it was drugs—cocaine and crack. Gravano's crew used to deal the stuff, but Gravano really didn't like his boys partaking in it, at least not heavily. DeBatt got hooked pretty badly and the drugs started to have an effect on his personality, causing bizarre behaviour. He developed paranoia and took to holing up in his house and keeping watch at the front window, waiting with loaded gun for an imaginary hit. In DeBatt's unsound mind, no one was going to get him without a fight.

DeBatt was becoming a liability, and as a rule, the mob doesn't put up with that kind of thing for long.

### OLD FRIENDS

Allegedly, it was Gravano himself who arranged the hit. The old friendship that had supposedly existed between him and DeBatt was now irrelevant—DeBatt had to go. On November 2, 1987, after attending a wedding, DeBatt came back to his restaurant. There he was murdered in front of the bar, his body left to cool by the orange electric light of the jukebox.

And that should be the end of the story, but it's not. It's said that the spirit of Michael DeBatt still haunts the place where he was gunned down. From time to time a ghostly voice can be heard whispering the name "Mike", while phantom faces can be seen peering out of mirrors. Those who work there feel as if they are constantly being watched, as shadowy figures disappear down the basement stairs.

Who knows? Maybe it *is* DeBatt, trying to find a little peace and a little justice.

# WILFRED "WILLIE BOY" JOHNSON
## AUGUST 29, 1988

## STOOL PIGEON

For a very long time Wilfred "Willie Boy" Johnson played both sides of the fence. It must have been for sixteen years or so that he fed the FBI information while working for the Gambino family in John Gotti's crew. It's a considerable time to keep a secret like that under wraps. Maybe Johnson felt that the mob owed him something, and he was going to make darn sure that they paid.

A pal of John Gotti's from a long way back, Johnson began to feed information to the FBI in around 1966. It was at that time that he went to prison on a robbery charge. During his stay in jail Johnson believed—in fact had been assured, apparently—that caporegime Carmine Fatico would provide for Willie's wife and children while he was away, make sure the family could pay their bills, want for nothing. That was the mob way, as Johnson understood it—a perk of being an associate. Fatico did no such thing and Johnson's wife was forced to go on welfare to make ends meet.

Once Johnson realized that Fatico had let him down, he started to look around a little bit, to see the world in a new light, and that included John Gotti. Though Johnson and Gotti were supposedly pals, Johnson began to feel that he had always been given second-hand jobs, the ones that nobody else wanted, and that he was being treated as little more than a gofer. Johnson also started to notice Gotti's slurs on his background. He was half Italian on his mother's side; his father was of Native American descent, either Mohawk or Cherokee (sources differ on this account). Maybe Gotti was just trying to be funny, but every so often he would refer to Johnson in less than savoury terms, all the while professing to be the man's friend. Johnson found it harder and harder to let these comments slide.

Yet despite this, and despite the fact that Johnson was basically ratting out the mob, he refused to actually testify against the Gambinos—that he just wouldn't do. For one thing, if he ever did testify against them, he knew his life would be over.

### A BAD PLAN

Things went along like this for quite a while until 1985, when John and Gene Gotti, Johnson and others were indicted on RICO charges. The authorities had been trying to build a case against Gotti for quite some time, and one prosecutor—Diane Giacalone—decided she wanted to use Johnson to bring the Don down. Giacalone's plan was to out Johnson as an informant. That way he would be forced to turn state's evidence in order to save his life. Afterward, he would be allowed into the Witness Protection Program. And Giacalone did just that, at least partly—she outed Johnson. He vehemently denied the accusations, but the cat was now out of the bag. Yet true to his promise to himself, Johnson refused to testify against Gotti.

Johnson was on his own then, with no WPP to guard him. On the morning of August 29, 1988, he was shot six times as he headed for his car to go to work. Hearing the shots, Johnson's wife ran from the house, but it was too late—he was dead. And after all of this, after Johnson's cover was blown and his life was forfeited, the prosecution's case against Gotti fell through. The Teflon Don was acquitted.

# 7 THE NINETIES TO TODAY: MODERN TIMES

**Cyber-crime, identify theft—organized crime is becoming ever more sophisticated. But have things really changed that much? In the end, it's still all about the money.**

But it is possible that as far as the Mafia itself is concerned, there has been a change, a shift in power. The families in New York, Chicago, LA and other big US cities are still formidable, but things are certainly stirring north of the border. It's just possible that there's more going on in Montreal, Toronto and Hamilton than the general public knows about. Let's hope that twenty-first-century law enforcement is on top of the situation.

# MARIO RICCOBENE
## JANUARY 28, 1993

### RICCOBENE'S REVENGE

Once an informer is safely ensconced in the Witness Protection Program, it isn't often that they exit it again. It's hard to know why someone would leave the safety of a fresh start, the security of a new home and a new job, just to make himself a target for the mob once more. Maybe certain people get bored if they don't have some sort of mob work to occupy their time, or perhaps they simply can't leave the old life behind. Mario Riccobene, it seems, was one of these.

In Philadelphia, the Scarfo/Riccobene war was over, and in a way both sides had lost. The Riccobenes were dead (Robert), in prison (Harry) or dispersed. The supposed winners of the war, the Scarfos, were in disarray and mob boss Nicodemo Scarfo had received a hefty prison sentence that lasts until 2033, which means he will die behind bars.

It was around this period—1984—that Mario Riccobene became an informant. He had suffered some heavy losses in the Philadelphia conflict—his brother, of course, but also his son Enrico, who wasn't even a member of the mob at all, but had been so disturbed by what was going on that he killed himself. Mario did some heavy soul-searching and decided it was time to get out of the family business. And for Mario, that meant not only testifying against the Scarfos—an act that he'd undoubtedly enjoy—but against his half-brother Harry too. Brother against brother. Mario's testimony helped put Harry away for good. Maybe that was a blessing in disguise for Harry, though, as he had spent so much time in jail he never really felt secure on the outside.

So Mario did the deed then entered the WPP. After that, he quietly slipped away somewhere and that should have been the end of the story. Except Mario Riccobene just couldn't say goodbye.

### BACK IN TOWN

Riccobene hadn't lasted very long in the WPP. He'd been expelled from it in 1989 after twice contacting people from his old life—a violation of the Program's rules. Maybe he missed the excitement of his old life, or maybe he was just lonely.

In any case, by 1992 Riccobene was in Philadelphia again, trying to get back into the swing of things—but everyone understood that he was really a walking corpse who just didn't know when it was time to lie down.

On January 28, 1993, as Riccobene was sitting in his Ford Taurus in a parking lot in New Jersey, a hit-man quietly sauntered up to his car and blew him away. Riccobene died just as he'd lived the last few years of his life—alone, and no doubt waiting to get in touch with an old friend. Because that's how the mob does it—nothing is as effective as getting friends and brothers to stab each other in the back.

# HERBERT "FAT HERBIE" BLITZSTEIN
## JANUARY 6, 1997

### THE HOLE IN THE WALL GANG

After the death of Anthony Spilotro, Herbert Blitzstein was like a man adrift and alone in a vast sea. Herbert, or "Fat Herbie", was in a tight spot. It might seem that a hulking figure of a man—6ft tall and over 300 pounds—would be capable, intimidating, able to leave his own unmistakable mark wherever he went, but Blitzstein, despite his size, had always been a wing-man, a wiseguy in the supporting cast rather than a featured player. Once Spilotro shuffled off, Blitzstein's rackets were basically up for grabs.

Blitzstein came from Chicago to Vegas with Spilotro, helping the mobster operate the Outfit's lucrative casino-skimming operations. Spilotro was the brains and Blitzstein was the very impressive muscle. Spilotro's group also ran a burglary ring—the Hole in the Wall Gang, so named because the members would enter an abode by busting out a hole in the side of the building.

Things were going well in Vegas for a while until Spilotro got himself blacklisted at the casinos and then the law came down pretty hard on not only Spilotro but the Outfit as well. Naturally enough the Chicago mob removed Spilotro from its register—permanently. After a stint in prison, then, Blitzstein was out on his own.

## BACK IN THE SADDLE AGAIN

Blitzstein made his way back to Vegas and seemed to be flying under the radar for a while. But the man—impeccably dressed and looking like a mobbed-up Luciano Pavarotti—couldn't be anything other than what he was and pretty soon he was running rackets again. Only this time, there was no Spilotro and no Outfit to back him up.

Blitzstein didn't help himself either, though. Bringing in some solid money from loansharking and fraud, he did not see fit to share it with the other powers operating in the free town of Vegas, including Los Angeles' Milano Brothers. This left him unguarded and open for anybody to take a poke at. And that, of course, is exactly what the Milanos did, with a little assistance from some goons from Buffalo.

The end came on January 6, 1997 when Herbie Blitzstein was found in his home, slumped over in a chair. At first glance it appeared that he had suffered a heart attack, but further investigation revealed that Blitzstein had been killed by a bullet, or three.

# GERLANDO SCIASCIA
## MARCH 19, 1999

### GEORGE FROM CANADA

The hit on Gerlando Sciascia was a delicate job, one that required finesse and subterfuge. One false step and the results could mean war—a bloody battle between the Bonanno family and the powerful Rizzutos of Canada. If it did come down to war, the repercussions would be international; the Rizzutos were an influential link to the Sicilian Mafia. Bonanno boss Joe Massino was well aware of all this, but as far as he was concerned he had no other choice—Sciascia had to go.

For a long time, outsiders regarded the Rizzutos as simply an offshoot of the Bonannos. The Montreal family funnelled kilos of narcotics into the United States via Canada and also ran some very lucrative rackets in Quebec and Ontario, but other than that, the Rizzutos were just a branch of one of New York's five families, not a power in their own right. That, however, was not the view held by Vito Rizzuto, who exercised significant authority in Montreal. As far as he was concerned the Rizzutos didn't need to rely on the waning influence of the Bonannos. Tall, handsome, dapper and imposing, Rizzuto was a born leader and as such was beholden to no one, not even Joe Massino.

Gerlando Sciascia was the liaison between the two families. Residing in Montreal for a while, Sciascia (also known as George from Canada) was a caporegime with the Bonannos. With contacts in both families, George was the perfect bridge between the two separate worlds—at least that's what Massino intended.

## FAMILY TIES

But there may have been a few things that hadn't occurred to Massino. Born in Sicily, Sciascia came from the same village that the Rizzutos hailed from. In the clannish world of the Mafia, close ties are everything.

Sciascia's true position became crystal clear when his second-in-command—Joseph LoPresti—was murdered. LoPresti was a Bonanno "made man", and no doubt pretty adept at keeping Massino up to date on Sciascia's comings and goings. LoPresti's murder hadn't been sanctioned by Massino and Sciascia's excuse was that he had been removed because of drug use. The careful Massino thought otherwise and began to reconsider the Sciascia situation.

The end came on March 19, 1999. Supposedly heading for a meeting, George from Canada was murdered, and his body unceremoniously dumped in the middle of a road somewhere. The intent was to make the killing look like a drug deal gone wrong.

But Vito Rizzuto wasn't buying it. His slick Machiavellian mind realized, or at least strongly suspected, what had really gone down that day in March. By the end of the 1990s the Rizzutos ceased funnelling money into the coffers of the Bonanno family; there would be no more tribute from Canada. The Montreal family had just solidified its formidable power.

# ADOLFO BRUNO
## NOVEMBER 23, 2003

## THE BAD GUYS

When you're a Mafia boss, whether a caporegime or a crew leader, you're always looking to see who's coming up behind you. It's a hard fact, but when you're at the top, there's invariably someone waiting to take your place, and willing to do anything to get there. The bottom line is that you can't trust anyone, especially the members of your own crew. Sometimes that's a lesson that's only learned in the last few moments of life, when it's too late.

That's the way it was for Adolfo Bruno, leader of the Genovese family's Springfield, Massachusetts crew. The bullets that took Bruno down had been bought and paid for by a man who had not only been a childhood friend of Bruno's son, but had been a protégé of Bruno's. Betrayals don't come more bitter than that.

The killer was Springfield crew member Anthony Arillotta, hungry for control of the crew. It was the usual mafioso social Darwinism—kill or be killed. Arillotta must have been waiting for quite a while to see off Bruno and his chance came when he stumbled upon an unsubstantiated report incriminating Bruno as an FBI informant. With this golden nugget of information, Arillotta went straight to Genovese acting boss Arthur Nigro. The evidence, such as it was, really wouldn't have stood up in a court of law, but then it didn't have to. The story only had to be good enough for Nigro.

## LAST HAND AT THE CLUB

Arillotta got the go-ahead, then. On November 23, 2003, Bruno spent a pleasant enough evening playing cards at a social club. It was the last evening Bruno would ever spend, pleasant or otherwise, for as the capo exited the club, a man stepped out of the bushes and shot him six times. Bruno fell dead in the parking lot and Arillotta became the boss of the Springfield crew.

Now here's the kicker, and it is pretty rich. In 2010, Arillotta was arrested for the murder of Bruno and in order to avoid grievous punishment, he immediately flipped—became an informant. Almost everyone who had anything to do with the killing of Bruno, from the actual triggerman to the guys who set up the hit and the top banana himself—Arthur Nigro—were brought down, the bulk of them getting life.

Arillotta was praised for being one of the "best" informants ever. Instead of lengthy imprisonment, he received a scant ninety-nine months (with time already served counting toward the total sentence) and a fine of two million dollars for planning Bruno's murder. Ninety-nine months and two million—that's how much Adolfo Bruno's life amounted to in the end. Sometimes the bad guys win; but hey, it's the mob. They're all bad guys.

# NICOLO RIZZUTO
## NOVEMBER 10, 2010

### VENDETTA IN MONTREAL

When Nicolo Rizzuto was assassinated in his Montreal home, he was eighty-six years old. The mob don't generally kill people in that age group; by and large they leave the "vulnerables" alone. Mothers, children, the aged—they're usually off limits. But the murder of Nicolo Rizzuto was a cut above the usual mob slaying; it was part of an overall assault on the Montreal family. As such, his death was meant to drive home the following message to Vito Rizzuto: "It's open season on the Rizzutos. No one is safe."

Two things precipitated this bloody power play. First, the position of Vito Rizzuto, Montreal's formidable mob boss, was compromised when he was extradited and sent to prison in the United States in 2007. He had been convicted for his role in the 1981 murder of the Three Capos—Philip Giaccone, Dominick Trinchera and Alphonse Indelicato.

The second factor was the deportation of the reputed acting head of the Bonanno family, Salvatore Montagna, from the United States into Canada. So Vito was sent to the United States, while Salvatore was shipped back to Canada. The situation now consisted of an out-of-work mob boss residing in Montreal, and a power vacuum in the Rizzuto family. The results were inevitable and devastating, especially for Vito.

It's alleged that once he arrived in Montreal Montagna got

right down to business. The first to go was Vito's son, Nick Junior, who was murdered in December of 2009, just eight months after Montagna had set foot in Canada. After that, bodies began to drop at an alarming rate, including Rizzuto's brother-in-law and culminating in the murder of Vito's father, Nicolo.

## THE ELDER RIZZUTO

Nicolo was no frail octogenarian; he was an active member of the family, a ruthless mafioso in his own right. Nicolo played the game like it was still the 1930s. That's what made his assassination all the more brazen. On November 10, 2010, Nicolo was killed while he was in his mansion, with his wife and daughter present. The hired gun entered the trees surrounding the Rizzuto stronghold and blasted through Nicolo's double-glazed windows, windows that were meant to act as armouring. For the Mafia, it doesn't get any worse than this. The murder of Nicolo Rizzuto was a flagrant affront; a declaration of war.

Vito had suffered much. In less than a year, he had lost both his son and his father. Though he would not be released from prison until 2012, he would not wait to exact his revenge. Very soon Montreal's underworld understood the nature of his vendetta.

# SALVATORE MONTAGNA
## NOVEMBER 24, 2011

### THE BODY IN THE WATER

What a story—murder mob-style, betrayal, more murder. And the ending? Well, for Salvatore Montagna, the end came when he was face down in the icy waters of L'Assomption River. Moments before, Montagna had been very much alive, running for his life through the trees of a northern Montreal suburb. His plan, born of desperation, had been to fling himself into the river and swim across to the opposite shore. But a single bullet put paid to that idea, and he only made it as far as the shoals. That was it for Montagna.

In the violent realm of the Montreal underworld, a bloody battle had been raging for several years. Mob boss Vito Rizzuto, godfather of the Montreal family, was in prison in the United States, and had left a vacant chair. Vito's brother-in-law, son and father had been killed and the foundations of the Rizzuto family had been shaken from forces both within and without. And it was allegedly Montagna who had been the cause of most of this.

Montagna had been termed the acting boss of the Bonanno family, and was one of the youngest bosses ever. At just 36, he was referred to by the press as the Bambino Boss, and he had a seat on the Commission. But in 2009, Montagna refused to become an informant and as a Canadian citizen, he found himself deported back to Montreal. And that's when all the trouble started in Quebec.

Apparently Montagna was not alone in all this excitement; allegedly he also had Montreal native Raynald Desjardins to help him.

### BIKER BUDDIES

Desjardins was a tough customer. He'd been a friend of Vito Rizzuto—a very close friend at one time. He and Rizzuto had lived on the same street together, and Desjardins had supposedly worked as the Rizzuto liaison to the Hell's Angels.

And this is where the betrayal comes in. It appears that Desjardins decided to take advantage of the weakened condition of his old friend Vito and to strike while the iron was hot. With the backing of Montagna, and the latter's connections to New York, the timing could not have been better. So in short order, Montagna and Desjardins apparently worked on reducing the numbers of the powerful Rizzutos, who had an empire worth billions and mob connections all over the world.

But something went terribly wrong. In the murky world of the Mafia nothing is ever written down, so just what happened is anybody's guess. In any case, in September of 2011 Desjardins found himself the target of an unsuccessful assassination attempt. Evidently Montagna and Desjardins were no longer the best of pals.

It's dog eat dog in the mob, so retaliation has to be swift. With Vito Rizzuto sitting in jail in Colorado and ordering the elimination of everyone who had been involved in the death of his loved ones, Desjardins decided he'd do his bit and get his own back on his friend from New York.

And that's how Salvatore Montagna ended up face down in the icy waters of L'Assomption. At the time of writing, though Desjardins has pleaded guilty to conspiracy in the murder of

Montagna, he has yet to be sentenced. Very few charges have actually been laid, and all of the above is only alleged. It remains to be seen what the courts have to say with regard to Desjardin's role in this. Hold onto your hats though—the battle for Montreal is a current event.

# INDEX

# PICTURE CREDITS